From Jersey To Me:

The Awakening & Healing of a Goddess

Wendi Dennine Cherry

From Jersey To Me: The Awakening & Healing of a Goddess

The content of this book is for general informational purposes only. It is not meant to be used, nor should it be used, to diagnose or treat any medical condition or to replace the services of your physician or other healthcare providers. The advice and strategies contained in the book may not be suitable for all readers. Please consult your healthcare provider for any questions that you may have about your medical situation. Neither the author, publisher, IIN nor any of their employees or representatives guarantee the accuracy of information in this book or its usefulness to a particular reader, nor are they responsible for any damage or negative consequence that may result from any treatment, action taken, or inaction by any person reading or following the information in this book.

I do not own the rights to any of the music.

Table of Contents

Reviews

I was immediately drawn to Wendi as a friend almost a decade ago and I completely understand why now. Her thoughtful approach to lessons learned in love and life while being transparent on trials and tribulations is refreshing. The variety of music woven throughout her story had me reminiscing on parts of my own story.
-Dy Brown, Advocacy Executive

The level of transparency and truth that Wendi puts into this book is inspiring. From Jersey To Me allows people who are connected to Wendi to understand her truth even more. This book also allows the reader, no matter who they are, to reflect on their level of self-honesty as they move towards a path of wholeness and increased health.
-Kayenecha Daugherty, Music Industry Executive

After I read this book, I felt moved, motivated, and inspired! Your relatable and personable writing, made me feel like I was with you as you encountered all of the amazing people from your toolkit. Not only did you share these spiritual experiences, but you also made your readers feel that these changes were attainable for us as well. So many women are lost and broken but often feel that there is no way to change their circumstances. Thanks for being a tool in all of our toolkits!
-Carmel Domond, Educator

I love the ease with which Wendi shares her story of transformation from wandering through life to creating her best life. She indeed is an example of how women can regain their feminine power to heal everything that ails them. This book gives detailed input on ways to use the tools you have to create the life you desire.
-Dr. Jeri Dyson, Physician

From Jersey to Me is great storytelling; the imagery and nostalgia illustrated in this narrative speaks directly to our shared and nuanced coming of age experiences as Black girls in the US and strong family roots that grow from the heart. We all have to navigate the concrete and fundamental roots of who we are and Wendi's journey is beautifully expressed here.
-Candace Jones, Producer, Project Director

Written in a very relatable way! All women readers can vehemently shake our heads in agreement throughout this book! It is so special and will give you great vibes. You will be drawn in and want to read more!
-Tessa Murphy, Business Analyst

"Short, emotion-packed chapters that are page-turners. I put the book down twice in one chapter because the emotion is so real and the stories are so intense. Wendi puts it all on the table and the liberating energy she conveys to the reader feels infectious"
-Tiffanee Neighbors, Author, Entrepreneur

Wendi Cherry is as real as it gets and exemplifies the triumph of the human spirit! As she transitions from ignoring her innate intuition to liberating herself, her healing journey was messy and beautiful. She is a true inspiration!
-Dr. Hanisha Patel, Naturopathic Physician

Wendi painted a vivid picture of her experiences. I could feel her pain and joy and found her raw honesty and openness to be the most effective parts of her story. Her vulnerability and courage really shine through which make her relatable and made me root for her.
-Troy Pinckney, Editor, Producer

Dedication

Dear Boogie,

Thank you for helping me grow. May you remember to always show up as the smart, beautiful, witty, intuitive, and loving Goddess you were born to be.

Love, Mommy

This book is dedicated to my mom who has always loved, nurtured, and taken care of me and ALWAYS has my back.

This book is dedicated to the women who have overcome immeasurable obstacles to survive. I pray this memoir inspires and empowers you to unapologetically transform into your most authentic and healthy self, by tapping into the Goddess within.

Acknowledgments

Thank you to The Sibs Nation for all of your support: Aimee (Aimee Dawn), Lisa (Almightee), Cher (Widdle Big), Erinn (Stis), Shannon (Shan Shan), Shawn (Shawnie Pooh), Summer (Baby Sum Sum), and Chers.

Thank you to all of my Sister-Friends and my Delta Sigma Theta, Inc. Sorors for your encouragement, there are too many to name but you know who you are.

Special thanks to my content editors Candace, Carmel, Dy, Dr. Gina, Dr. Hanisha, Dr. Jeri, Jones, Janaye, Kayenecha, M'Bwebe, Tiffanee, Tessa, and Troy who made me dig deeper to tell my story.

Special thanks to the people who have intentionally and unknowingly poured into my life.

Dr. Nazirakh Amen, Anthony Browder, Dr. John Henrik Clarke, Auset Eyowaku, Lisa Marie Goodson, Dr. Vikki Johnson, Risikat 'Kat' Okedeyi, Dr. Gina Paige, Jawanza Kalonji Rand, Thema Azize Serwa, Dr. Zoe Spencer, Dr. Sakiliba Mines, Dr. Patricia Newton, Mayasa Telfair, Ericka Totten, Dr. Josef Ben Yochanan, and the countless others who have contributed to my evolution.

Warning: Contains explicit language.

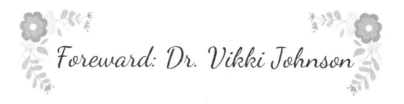

Foreward: Dr. Vikki Johnson

The entire purpose of life is to find out why you were born. What were you sent here to do? Who are you destined to be? What is your story? What lessons have you learned? Who do you get to be now that you have learned a few things? I have known Wendi for many years now. She is gracious, smart, inquisitive, spiritual, health-conscious, awakening, and committed to leaving an indelible imprint on the world.

I have witnessed her transformation. I am still holding space for her whirlwind life experiences because they bring me great joy and they bring her contentment, fulfillment, enlightenment. It is an awesome privilege to watch her manifest her "divine feminine self" and then choose to want other women to have the same experience. She is blessed. Her daughter is blessed. Her sisters are blessed. Her mothers are blessed. Her friends are blessed. Her Delta Sigma Theta Sorors are blessed. Mother Nature is blessed because Wendi Cherry IS always on her way to something better.

In her book, ***From Jersey to Me: The Awakening & Healing of a Goddess***, Wendi takes us all on her journey of experience, education, evolution, and expansion. This book reads much like a journal or a personal diary. It is a page-turner. It leaves you wanting to know what happens next. It will make you reflect on your childhood and the times you thought you knew everything but knew nothing. The whimsical invisibility we all had as children than teens than young adults and for some of us still as "full-grown humans" has put all of us at one time or another in some awkward situations. Her transparency will trigger some pain, some joy, some tears, some laughter, some compassion, and some ahas. Her candor unlocks memories of times past, present opportunities, and future possibilities.

At the end of this book, you will either cower from the thought of becoming a risk-taker like Wendi OR you will feel a spark of courage that ignites your soul in a way that leaves you drenched with gratitude. Either way, you will take a trip from somewhere to somewhere else...even if only in your imagination. Hopefully, however, her journey will provide a road map for every reader to become more self-aware of their divinity.

The best is yet to come!

Dr. Vikki Johnson
Chaplain, Speaker, Author,
& Creator, Soul Wealth®
www.vikkijohnson.com

I AM

Tisha Renee: The name the nurses in the hospital gave me at birth.

Wendi Dennine: The name my parents gave me when they adopted me.

Kora: The name the Creator gave me when I asked *HER* what my purpose was.

Goyzam: The name given to me by the Ambassador of the Cameroonian Embassy, Ambassador Joseph Charles Bienvenu Foe-Atangana, meaning ***The Beloved One***.

Each one has a different persona and I can switch between them depending on the situation. They are all walking with me on this journey #FromJerZtoMe. All of my experiences from growing up in a loving adopted family, to reconnecting with my biological family, to tracing my DNA back to Cameroon (Maternal side | Mafa Tribe) and Sierra Leona (Paternal side | Temne Tribe) and Germany, are shaping me and preparing me for my GOD-ordained destiny and purpose.

I've had one or three sleepless nights trying to figure out how much or little to share in this book. It is certainly a long time coming, my experiences are so vast and I can't share everything. So, I have intentionally selected specific experiences offering *MY* perspective. There are many sides to every story so, this just happens to be *MY* side, from *MY* experience, from *MY* memory. If it resonates with you, wonderful, if it doesn't, eat the meat and throw away the bones. I am **NOT** attempting to convert you to any one way of being.

After each chapter, I have included journaling prompts for you to journal your thoughts and feelings. This book contains my stories and some of the tools I used to navigate some very tough situations. During the process of documenting my life, I came to understand that it can be difficult to say the right thing to make sure that everyone who has been a part of my experiences has their feelings preserved. There is no judgment for anyone else and most importantly for myself. As I've matured, I now understand that we did the best that we could in those specific situations, with the information and resources we had at the time.

If this information does not apply to you, it should not trigger you in any way. However, if it does trigger you, then there may be an opportunity for you to explore, using your own, unfiltered intuition, what you are feeling on a deeper level.

Though I remain clear that the work of awakening and healing remains in the mirror, having a support system has been critical to my evolution, these *guides* held space for me, both directly and indirectly, when I couldn't hold it for myself, and I am full of gratitude.

Ultimately, I created this work because…

1. I believe everyone has the right to share their *own* stories from their perspectives.

2. It helps me heal, sort of like therapy - which I have had a lot of and which I suggest to everyone.

3. It shows the perspective of a successful, well-adjusted, melanated woman who has **chosen** to triumph over all of her adversities.

4. My intention is to educate, inspire, and empower melanated women to unapologetically transform into their most authentic and healthy selves, by tapping into the Goddess within.

Thank you for joining me on this journey From Jersey to Me!

Reflection Journal & Guided Meditations

Over the years, I realized that what I considered a 'good' or 'bad' experience was merely my perception. Ultimately, I have never really lost anything, instead I choose to believe I have gained, through sometimes painful, incredible life lessons. I remain clear that unpacking what the lessons meant is the work that has to be done by each of us, while standing in the mirror. I've been blessed to have powerful guides to encourage my development and to hold space for me when I couldn't hold it for myself. I want to pay it forward by providing the same sanctuary and safe space for you, here in these pages.

My recommendation is that you allow yourself plenty of quiet time to complete the questions after reading each chapter. This will keep the message from the chapter at the fore-front of your mind and in your spirit. However, don't put pressure on yourself to complete everything after your first read of the book. The intention is not to add something new to your 'to-do' list, but to offer you a place to reflect and document your own process of awakening and healing. If you have never considered this type of self-excavation and discovery before, you can consider this a blueprint and the first step of a life-long journey to becoming your most healthy and authentic self.

My Lessons & Discoveries

After each chapter, I will provide commentary on the lessons that I learned through some of my most challenging and life-changing experiences. I will compare my thought process back then, with how I currently navigate situations, based on the new tools and information I acquired along my journey of awakening and healing.

Journaling Prompts

My mother introduced me to journaling in 1978. I have shifted what, as a young girl, was simply a hobby of documenting what was happening between me, my family, and friends, into a full-blown tool of manifestation. Not only a tool of manifestation, but reflection, healing, and mostly gratitude for having documented and being a witness to my own amazing evolution thus far.

- At the end of each chapter, I have provided journaling prompts for you to reflect on the lesson you may have learned from a specific chapter.

- The journaling prompts will encourage you to write down your thoughts because writing provides you with more clarity and focus.

- If any of the information in this book causes a trigger from one of your past experiences, I suggest seeking out a qualified therapist or coach to support you while you unpack your feelings.

- This book is meant for you to begin the conversation within yourself. If you run out of space in the lines provided, get a journal or notebook to continue to fully flesh-out your thoughts, aha moments, and vision for the future.

1. Exercises

At the end of the book there will be a few exercises to get you started on discovering and setting your own intentions, to reflect on where you would like to go next on your journey, and the next steps to support your vision.

2. Mantras & Meditations

I have found that guided meditations help keep me focused during my quiet time. They don't have to be long and drawn out just intentional and clear.

The Awakening

I Was Kidnapped by The Police

"Turn around and put your hands behind your back!" the officer snarled at my mother and me. I complied, not wanting to be amongst the statistics of other melanated (I prefer this description as "black" is not a nation but merely a color. It refers to people with black and brown skin of African or indigenous descent) human beings shot dead for questioning such an absurd, unwarranted gesture. Complicating the issue was my large, copper, Wonder Woman-style bangle on my wrist, hidden under my coat. The officer was unable to see it and had little patience to try to understand why his handcuffs weren't wrapping around my wrists with ease. I was trying to explain that the bangle was preventing him from using the handcuffs and that I would need to move my hands to remove it. "Do what you want," he spat at me. I told him I was making him clear of my next move so he wouldn't shoot me, right there, on the spot. After I removed it, he proceeded to hand-cuff me directly in front of my then 10-year-old daughter, who was frozen, staring at me in horror.

Now, I had been stopped by the cops for speeding on many occasions. My dad used to call me "Lead Foot" for my love of putting the pedal to the metal, but I had never been arrested or treated so poorly before. The music from the movie, Mississippi Burning, started playing in my head as soon as the four cop cars and two ambulances converged on the scene, with their sirens blaring, in Atlantic Highlands, New Jersey, nonetheless. What a joke! It was clear that this clown posse wasn't pulling up to protect and serve. The year was 2011, and due to social media and camera phones, worldwide, the true colors of particular groups of people were exposed. In the United States, since colonization, this has been the course of treatment of melanated people. What was happening to my mom, and I was no exception.

Things were becoming more publicly volatile as Trayvon Martin was murdered just two months later, as were countless, nameless others. I had no idea how to articulate how I was feeling, other than tired, viscerally angry, worn out, and just plain sad. Over the years, I had not given into the boiling emotions I'd been suppressing internally since 2nd grade. Yep, you read that right, 2nd grade. These occurrences brought me back to my very first experience with racism that I can remember. This particular incident happened during an overnight trip at Camp Sacajawea with my Girl Scout troop. While attempting to go to sleep, the other girls, who happened to be all white, decided to look for something "bad" to do. There I was, all cozy in *my* damn sleeping bag, minding *my* damn business, flicking *my* damn flashlight on and off, when I heard a certain girl say, "Let's ask Wendi what to do, she's black, so she knows about "bad" stuff." I shot up, blinked, then laid back down as I scanned the room realizing that the majority of my fellow Scouts were looking at me with high expectations to come up with something "bad" to do. I was dazed, offended, and pissed all at the same time, so I slunk down and covered my face with my sleeping bag, signaling the first of countless times I would push down my true feelings.

I was ready for a revolution, and since I didn't have control over anyone else, it took me a while, but I was coming to grips with the fact that **the revolution had to begin with me**. The first step was to find out who I was and what I wanted. Next, I began to heal myself from past traumas and issues I never even knew I had. Talk about painful...wow! Then, I surrounded myself with a tribe of people who help keep me on track and have permission to call me out on my occasional poor decisions. It took many years and lots of work for me to get my 'ish' together. What I wasn't prepared for was the level of self-hatred and fear of rejection that I was harboring – that was the hardest part of the work. The hatred manifested itself in my lack of ability to speak my truth, to stand up for myself, to consider my feelings above all else, to trust my intuition. I had noticed that these actions had become my modes operandi, throughout my life, and I was ready for something new.

The experience of being arrested awakened me out of my slumber. It became the catalyst for me to heal my long-held wounds to finally unapologetically become the powerful co-creator and Goddess I was born to be. This change of mindset and intention began to take form after I learned more about myself, freed myself from old thought patterns, and value systems that had held me down for decades. I finally got still and allowed my Ancestors and The Creator to guide me!

I'm so happy to say my life has changed in ways I never thought possible. I feel freer and more connected to spirit than ever before. I hope the stories in this book inspire you to take stock of your life, honestly decide if you are living your best life at this moment, if not, that you identify what is stopping you, and what steps you need to change it. I am merely sharing these personal accounts as inspiration for you, the reader to unapologetically transform into your most authentic and healthy version by tapping into the God/dess within; in whatever way, shape or form, that means for you.

Chapter 1: Selected Not Expected

"The development of the child during the first three years after birth is unequaled in intensity and importance by any period that precedes or follows in the whole life of the child." — Maria Montessori

*L*et's start from the beginning, shall we?

From the time I was able to think and reason, I knew I was adopted at birth. I was born Tisha Renee in Elizabeth, NJ, in October 1970. My birth announcement read, ***"I Was Selected Not Expected!"*** I always knew that though I didn't come from my Mom's belly, I was special, loved, and wanted.

I was named Wendi Dennine after my parents. My Mom's name is Gwendolyn, and my dad's middle name was Denny. I wasn't fond of my middle name, and one day I asked my dad where the name "Denny" came from. With his familiar quick wit he shrugged and exclaimed, "Hell, I don't even know why my mother named me no damn Denny!" If nothing else, he had a great sense of humor. Over the years, I was made fun of because there weren't many melanated Wendy(s) walking around. That was considered a "white girl name" not to mention, Mommy was fancy with it and spelled mine W-e-n-d-i, with an "i" versus the traditional "y" at the end. When they built the fast-food restaurant Wendy's in my neighborhood, I thought I was cool. They had a policy that anyone named Wendi could get free Frosty ice cream and fries. Winning! However, on the other side of that was my last name, Cherry. As you can imagine, the kids had a field day because I got called all types of names, and if I had a dime for every time someone said "bust a Cherry," I'd be rich!

Being adopted was a natural part of my life, other than the kids at school trying to tease my sister and me about being "foster kids," I didn't overthink it. I knew there was "a woman" somewhere who was courageous enough to carry me to full-term and to give me up for adoption because she couldn't take care of me. The only real times it became an issue was when those same ignorant-assed kids teased my younger sister, Aimee, and me about our differences in color – she is dark-skinned, and I am light-skinned. Aimee was one year and a half younger than me, and since she was a kid, was a straight-shooter and not much for nonsense. She had curly black hair, chocolate skin, and what the grown-ups referred to as "big legs."

I had skinny legs, caramel-colored skin, and dry, sandy-colored hair. I knew that I was adopted, so I didn't expect to look like my adopted family. However, I did wonder if there was anyone else that looked like me. Did they have the same eye and skin color as me? *This* doo-doo brown, frizzy hair that naturally lightened by the summer sun? Did they occasionally pass out like me? As a child, I was both content and curious about "where I came from." Growing up in a small town, I frequently saw families where everyone looked exactly alike, I kind'a felt like an astronaut, with no gravity, freely spinning around in outer space, wrestling with that timeless question, that many humans ask themselves - "Who am I?"

Mommy, Aimee & Me!

My dad bounced on us when I was four, and then it became *Mommy, Aimee & Me*! Mommy made it fun, though, she never let on how hard it was raising two daughters as a single woman. When the furnace broke down, or the pipes burst in our house, that was just a reason for Aimee and me to sleep in Mommy's room...a rare treat! We had everything we needed *and* wanted, all of the love, hugs, kisses, toys, nurturing, and fun. We also had two dogs, two rabbits, and some fish as pets. One time to the chagrin of Mommy, ole' Aimee Dawn won a rabbit in a raffle from the Monmouth Mall. So, on the spot, she had to buy a cage, food, and other rabbit crap. All of our friends loved spending the night at our house because Mommy had candy, snacks and was renowned for her huge pancakes and egg, ham, and cheese sandwiches. She even kissed everyone before they went to bed.

My dad made occasional visits and one Christmas night, showed up late, to give Aimee and me each a toy Hess gas station truck as a gift. Though I politely accepted it, inside I knew that he hadn't taken the time to select an appropriate gift for us. These trucks were mere after-thoughts, which in my opinion, set the theme for our relationship moving forward. He was rather elusive for the majority of my childhood and only became aware of his presence after he'd snuck by, when we weren't home, to slip his minuscule child support check in the mailbox. His handwriting reminded me of an architect because he wrote in all capital letters. Since my dad left at such an early age, I didn't think I missed him. I knew I was loved - Mommy, Grandmommy, Granddaddy, Auntie & Uncle George made sure of that. I would, however, learn later that my dad's absence affected my life in ways that I couldn't have imagined.

Our house was always calm, peaceful, filled with love, and laughter. Mommy, Aimee, and I would hang out in the living room together, watching TV, eating, or listening to music. When we were younger, Aimee and I shared a room with bunk beds, and the extra room served as our playroom, complete with toys, games, and even an air hockey table. Mommy always had the newest items, including the earliest version of the video game called Pong, like tennis, you hit the ball from one side of the screen to the other. Later, we graduated to the big leagues and copped that Atari console with the joysticks. Every chance we got, she would take us to the museums, festivals, movies, restaurants, and the beach, including the water slide on the boardwalk in Long Branch, New Jersey. All of the kids loved coming to our house to play. Saturdays were pretty routine, we vacuumed and dusted the house before jumping in the shower just in time to catch "Soul Train" while putting on our lotion and clothes. After we'd head out to the store, and each of us would get a stack of coupons to make the grocery shopping go by faster.

Music is Life

Mommy was big on exposure. In 1975, she and her first cousin, who we called, Aunt Sylvia, took my cousin, Wanda and me to see the seven-time Tony Award-winning play, *The Wiz*, at the Majestic Theatre on Broadway in New York City. This particular trip was one of the most memorable, and even though I was only five, I remember it like it was yesterday. Not only because it was my first Broadway show, but it was also my first train ride into the Big Apple, and the first time a particular body of music so moved me, *The Wiz* the original cast's recording soundtrack.

From the opening tornado scene to the yellow brick road, played by men wearing gold afro wigs, to the beautiful costumes and the energy of the melanated people on that stage, I was captivated. Ted Ross earned his Tony Award playing the role of the Cowardly Lion. Even though he scared the crap out of me, I was intrigued by how the angelic and melodic voice of 16-year-old Stephanie Mills singing Charlie Small's composition, "Be a Lion," could change the demeanor from a scary to a friendly and courageous lion.

The highlight was the whole cast singing, what came to be my favorite song of the entire show, "Everybody Rejoice." Written by singer and songwriter Luther Vandross, the powerful lyrics of the song almost brought me to tears.

"Everybody be glad...because the sun is shining just for us!"

"Everybody wake up…into the morning into happiness!

"Can you feel a brand-new day?"

I loved that music so much that Mommy bought us the vinyl album, and I played it every day, devouring the liner notes and learning all of the lyrics. I wanted to know who this Luther Vandross and Stephanie Mills were and how come their songwriting and voices could invoke such emotion in my spirit. From there, I made it a habit to read the liner notes of each album cover we bought. In nursery school, I even performed "Be a Lion" during Show and Tell for my classmates. I remember I got all dressed up, and Mommy also sprayed some of her perfume on me for good luck! I can visualize myself standing before the class, singing my heart out, dead serious…

"…And with no fear inside…"

"No need to run, no need to hide…"

"You're standing strong and tall…"

"You're the bravest of them all…"

I ignored the side-eyes I was getting from my five-year-old classmates and focused on Mrs. Joan Nye, my first teacher at the Winding Brook Nursery School, who was standing there rooting me on. After the performance, she was the first to clap. When she noticed me rushing to take my seat on the floor, she insisted that I come back to the front of the class to take my curtsy.

The Wiz experience was my first indication that music held power and could affect my feelings. We loved it so much that Mommy still has the show's album and playbill in her basement.

Fight the Power

In January of 1977, while I was in first grade, Mommy guided me through—watching all nine-hours and 48 minutes of the gut-wrenching premiere of Alex Haley's "Roots," chronicling the history of Kunta Kinte, an African man kidnapped and sold into slavery in America. Being viscerally impacted, and not having the language for what I was feeling at that time, I knew that what had happened was wrong, and it made me sad.

I couldn't fathom that someone wouldn't like me just because of the color of my skin. I was outraged at the images on the screen of people being whipped, mistreated, chased, and killed simply because they had brown skin, like me. This experience was the catalyst that heightened my awareness around the issues of race; it was when I became conscious of the fact that I was a little melanated girl and some people may not like me because of it.

That next Christmas, while making my list for Santa in the local Toys R Us, I saw the famed Baby Alive doll in a box on the shelf. She was the hot ticket that year, because she could eat, pee, and poop! The picture on the front of the box was of a white doll with blue eyes; however, splashed across the front of the box were the words "black" written in bold type. There were rows of the white doll, and yet there was only one single box of the black baby. At such a young age, that still struck me as odd so, I asked Mommy how come they just hadn't put a picture of a black baby on the box. What was the big deal that the baby inside of the box was "black"?

I had so many questions, and since Mommy didn't have the answers, she suggested that I write a letter to the company and ask them myself. So, we sat down and wrote a letter asking those exact questions. Honestly, I don't remember if they had any valid response, and even more disappointing was that they had the nerve to send us a coupon for another Baby Alive doll. Though their response was inadequate, in my seven-year-old heart, I felt empowered to ask the hard questions, for this was the exact moment of planting the seed of my desire to advocate for melanated people.

The Power of Music

Music was always in our home, and some of my warmest memories are of Mommy, Aimee, and me dancing in our living room. Mommy was an early-adapter of electronics and gadgets, and I remember the first time she tested transferring the song "Second Time Around" by Shalamar from her 8-track tape to a cassette. When we realized it had worked, the three of us cheered and danced some more. We always had family and friends over, Aunt Sylvia and Wanda would come over on Fridays to listen to music and hang out. Us kids would run back and forth between the rooms, but when the beat dropped, we would run to the living room to do the dances we'd seen on "Soul Train" and "Solid Gold". I loved watching Mommy and Aunt Sylvia dance; they had moves for sure. When they heard a song they liked, Mommy would say, Heeeyyy!", and Aunt Sylvia would say, "Hooooo!" That meant the music was good to them!

Like clockwork, as soon as Wanda arrived, we'd convene in the back room, debating and plotting the precise time to strike with the inevitable, million-dollar question - "Can Wanda spend the night?" Ninety-percent of the time, the answer was yes. As cousins do, after the excitement wore off, Wanda and I would start fussing; most of those tiffs came when we were designing a "show" to share with the adults. Wanda thought because she was the oldest that she could boss Aimee and me around. Aunt Sylvia was not pleased and would remind us that we were cousins and were supposed to get along. Since we were always fighting each other, she called us the "Two Black Snakes" because we were in love with each other one minute then at each other's throats, the next. Nevertheless, because Aimee, Wanda, and I all loved to perform, we'd work together to create a skit and choreography, complete with wardrobe. Despite the fighting, the show had to go on.

We were multi-talented, and our skits usually contained song and dance numbers. One time we presented a fashion show, and since most real models had big boobs, we substituted egg-shaped plastic containers from Aunt Sylvia's Legg's brand stockings to place in our shirts for the full effect. However, there was a slight issue in that we only had two complete sets with one shell missing from the third set. As the elders, Wanda and I each got a set and in the spirit of not allowing a minor wardrobe malfunction to ruin our show. Poor Aimee placed her one shell in the center of her shirt, like a unicorn. Once the adults gave us the signal that it was the right time to make our entrance; usually, it was Aimee who would say, "Intro-duuu-ciiing..." and that was our cue to come from the wings and give 'em all we had. We had great taste because we'd learned from the best, so our song selection was on point with tracks from Quincy Jones' album *The Dude* or "The Best of My Love" by The Emotions. Once done, we'd always get a rousing round-of-applause and lots of praise from our parents, which pumped us up to begin to choreograph the next performance.

It was the era of Disco and Rhythm & Blues (R&B), and Mommy had all of the cool, vinyl albums. New York City was the number one media market in the world and exposed us to the hottest and newest joints of the day. Our green '72 Chevy only had an AM radio, so we jammed to some of the 70's soft rock's greats like Ambrosia, Chicago, Steely Dan, The Doobie Brothers, and Daryl Hall & John Oates. Flowing through the speakers in our house was *107.5 WBLS* and *98.7 KISS FM*, who played Luther Vandross and Change, Ashford and Simpson, Sylvester, Earth Wind & Fire, The Brothers Johnson, and the S.O.S Band. That music, along with the smooth voice of radio personality, "The Chief Rocker" Frankie Crocker, became the soundtrack to my youth with his number one show in the nation. Every chance I got, I would dig through my Mom's vinyl collection to devour the liner notes. The horns, the drums, the bass, the soulful voices of these singers always made me feel so light and free.

Between Mommy, Aunt Sylvia, and their other first cousin, Aunt Faye, they kept the dance floor smoking. Almost every other weekend, we'd hang out with Aunt Faye and Uncle Al along with our other cousins, Rodney and Erika. My God-Parents, Uncle Bobby and Aunt Delores, had a large basement where my God-Sisters, Cheryl and Jordan, along with our other family's friends, Necee and Tracie, made plenty of tents and forts. As kids, we always had a lot of fun downstairs while our parents would be upstairs partaking in the adult shenanigans. I still remember hearing lots of hoots and hollers coming from them. They would be cracking jokes, teasing each other, and talking about life! From my kid's perspective, there was always laughter, jokes, food, music, and most of all, safety. As we got older, we graduated to going to the Eatontown Roller Skating Rink, where we would spend our Saturdays at the first and second sessions. I always thought Cheryl and Jordan were so cool because they had black skates, and I had the regular white ones with the purple pom-poms. Sometimes Jordan, my very first "road-dog" and I would try to skate fast and maybe once-in-a-while, try to knock someone over. Those were some of the most fun times in my life.

I Said A Hip Hop...

Though I loved Mommy's music, I was beginning to develop a taste of my own. The musical climate was changing, and I was excited to explore these new sounds. I was eight-years-old when I purchased my very first album, *Off the Wall* by Michael Jackson. I'd just seen him in the movie version of *The Wiz*, and I knew he was the big brother of Penny from the sitcom, "Good Times." My two girlfriends, Aisha and Lethea, and I loved it so much that we decided to make up a dance to the song, "Working Day and Night" for the school talent show. We practiced our steps in my living room for hours. The Rock was the hottest dance at the time, named after another song from Michael's album – "Rock With You." So, there we were, rocking from side to side, one...two...one...two, then we got a bit tricky with it and added the four-corners moves. We repeated the same steps, side-to-side, then four-corners for the entire four minutes and 19 seconds of the track. Once the rehearsal ended, Mommy asked, "Aren't y' all going to add anything else to the dance?" "Hmmm, nope...", we replied. I mean between our dance moves, which we had "down-pat" and wardrobe selection of cornrows with beads, white tops, blue skirts, and white stockings - you couldn't tell us nothing. Of course, we killed it at the talent show.

Mommy was the one who introduced me to hip hop. It was 1979, and while we were having lunch with some neighborhood children in our dining room, she rushed in, telling us to settle down and listen to the sounds coming from the radio. I heard the background music and instantly thought, "I already know this song – it's Chic," who I loved, by the way. Their song "Good Times" was one of the most popular dance tunes of the time and provided the background music for this new song. I thought meh, I know this already so kind' a tuned out for a bit until I heard the infamous...

"I said-a hip, hop, a hippie to the hippie..."

"To the hip hip hop-a you don't stop..."

"The rocking, to the bang-bang boogi..."

"Say up jump the boogie to the rhythm of the boogie the beeeeat!"

That familiar beat and those unique lyrics coupled with this new style of music had all of us kids in complete silence, over our hot dogs and beans. For the next seven minutes, we sat mesmerized, listening intently. We had to know who "sang" that song! In perfect timing, the radio announcer said that this was a new song called "Rapper's Delight" by the Sugarhill Gang. Mommy went on to tell us that this style was called rapping, and people in her generation used to sit out on the stoop and sing-speak like that. She said that it reminded her of an old Disc Jockey (DJ) named Jocko.

Whatever it was, we were hooked and couldn't wait to hear it again. Back then, there were no on-demand media; you had to wait until the song came back on the radio. So, in an attempt to stay ready, Aimee and I put a cassette tape in the deck ready to press record as soon as we heard it again. Once we captured it on tape, we proceeded to learn every lyric by playing it for a few bars, then writing the words down, then rewinding it to ensure it was correct, then moving on to the next chunk. It took us about an hour or so to finish it, but then we were able to learn the words, sing along, and look cool to our friends.

This new genre of music called hip hop slowly but surely gained traction over the next few years, even though it took until 1983 for

'BLS to regularly play it with the debut of Supa Rockin' Mr. Magic's "Rap Attack," a show devoted *exclusively* to hip hop.

I was hooked and tuned in every chance I got. Every day after school, I would tune into DJ Ralph Mc Daniels on "Video Music Box." It was the first-ever music video show dedicated to hip hop. The show aired videos from Malcolm McLaren & The World-Famous Supreme Team, Big Daddy Kane, KRS One and Boogie Down Productions, Grandmaster Flash and the Furious Five, Run DMC, Eric B. and Rakim, and more. The lyrics, the beat, the style of dress, the energy of the whole movement just captured my soul – I couldn't get enough. I was always in awe of these young black and brown kids. Even though they grew up in the struggle, they still created an entire culture and movement that changed the world to become the most impactful musical genre that was *ever* created.

New York radio was so eclectic in the early 80's. It was not uncommon to hear Chicago's house music classic "Set it Off" by Strafe or the sound of euro pop acts like, Tears for Fears' "Shout" and Spandau Ballet's "True", on the same station. I loved it all!

The Original Master Teachers

Aimee and I spent our summers on the Eastern Shore of Virginia with *Grandmommy* (Mary Emma Jacobs Bailey), *Granddaddy* (John Arthur Bailey), Grandmommy's sister, affectionately known as *Auntie* (Margaret Sarah Jacobs Bailey), and Granddaddy's brother, *Uncle George* (George Edward Bailey). Would you believe that two brothers married two sisters? Growing up, I thought it was one of the coolest things ever. It was always a big deal for Aimee and me, aka 'The Jersey Birds' to arrive on the Eastern Shore. If school was out on June 20th by June 21st, we were heading down I-95 South, where we soaked up more love and attention, simply put, we were spoiled rotten. Talk about a carefree life!

We went to church every Sunday, Aimee went with Granddaddy to his family's church, Holy Trinity Baptist Church. I went with Grandmommy to Shiloh Baptist Church, which was less than one mile from Holy Trinity. Most Saturdays before church,

Grandmommy and Auntie, would travel far and wide to find just the right wine-colored shoes, to go with their new wine-colored pocketbook, and hat. It was not a game; those outfits had to be just right. When I turned five and joined the "Tot Choir," we scoured the entire Eastern Shore to find the perfect navy-blue skirt, white top, white stockings, and black patent leather shoes for the required uniform. This was in the old days when choirs still 'marched' up the aisles and into the choir stand. I remember the choir was so good; I loved to sing along and 'stand up and clap' when I heard a song I liked. I'd seen the older girls do it, so I copied their moves. In preparation for my choral debut, I practiced my march game all week; I'd twist from side to side, all the way through the living room and into the dining room of my grandparent's house. Back and forth, back and forth. For a while, I had studied the choir's cool moves, and this was my chance to shine. Therefore, I had to be on point.

This was also a big deal because it was the moment I got to wear my hair "out"! All little melanated girls remember the first time they got to wear their hair free from bows, braids, and barrettes. I loved going to Auntie's hair salon, also known as "the shop," to watch her put the grease on the back of her hand, put the curlers on the hot stove, and click-click-click the irons to style her customer's hair to perfection. The day before, my Tot Choir debut, she washed, straightened, then curled my long, dry, sandy brown hair until it was just right. I even got to wear one of her pretty, silk scarves to bed that night. Winning! The next morning, after a big breakfast of eggs, biscuits, orange juice, bacon, and grits, Granddaddy shined our patent leather shoes with ajax. Then he gave Aimee and me frozen peppermint patties and tissues for our pocketbooks.

The big day was here! The choir members gathered in the back of the church, to prepare to march. They lined everyone up in height order, which put me smack dab in the front of the line. Awh, yeah! I was ready! The second I heard Kenny Parker, the organist, hit his first note – I took-off down the aisle. Counting the steps in my head, chin up – rocking left, right, left, right, arms swinging like I'd seen Auntie do when she was "marching" to the choir stand ...in short, I was getting it! At that moment, an uproar of laughter took me out of my zone. I looked up only to see the entire church staring, pointing, and laughing at me. In my excitement, I'd taken off during the intro while the other choir members knew to wait for the chorus. I glanced over at Grandmommy who had loving tears of laughter in her eyes and sheepishly ran to the back of the church to try it again. After church everyone congratulated me telling me how well I'd done for my first time singing in the choir, I was hooked and would go on to sing in choirs for 30+ years after that. Though I was a little child, I loved how good the music at church made me feel, and I could tell it had the same effect on Grandmommy. Over the week, Grandmommy would cook, run her errands, and drive around humming the tune to the songs we'd just heard at Sunday service. Sometime I would catch her crying, which scared me. She always reassured me that she wasn't crying because she was sad but because she was 'happy'.

Though I loved going to church, I hated when Grandmommy used to "get happy." It was usually during the time the choir was singing. Her favorite song was *"In the Garden"*, *composed* by C. Austin Miles.

She would belt out…

"…and HE walks with me, talks with me and tells me I am HIS own."

"…and the joy we share as we tarry there, none other has ever known."

I think that was the way the song was written but then the organist, Kenny Parker, had to go and put his haunting and soulful spin on it. Oh, boy, that was all she wrote; I could feel the spirit coming over her because at first, she would start crying softly, and then twist up the handkerchief she was holding in her hand. This was the build-up, therefore, to distract her, I would ask her for a mint or if she could take me to the bathroom. She would ignore me, and one of the ladies sitting close to us would pull me away from her, probably for protection because that was right before she would, in the words of my cousin Wanda, "get to buck-dancing." This lasted until she ran out of energy, and then she would sit back down in her seat, rocking from side to side until she was fully calmed down. I did my best to stay as far away from her as I could. In those moments, I loved music but also was leery of the effect it had on Grandmommy. "How could one cry from being happy?", I wondered.

Granddaddy got dressed to the nines for his church services and because he served on the Deacon Board, and as a Trustee, he mainly wore black with white butler gloves. That didn't damper his love for fashion and clothes because he loved to get dressed up. He enjoyed modeling his clothes and hats for us. He was tall, loving, affectionate, and light-skinned with waves, a Hitler-styled mustache. My favorite things were when he let us hang from his arm muscles; I'd never seen muscles like that before except on the Popeye cartoon. After shaving, he would let me sit on his lap to put small pieces of tissue on the spots where he'd accidentally nicked himself. When opening a present, he would get a knife and very carefully and slowly open the box, attempting to preserve the paper, making a big production out of it. Frustrated, Aimee and I would say, "Come on, Granddaddy, can we just open it for you?!"

He was a long-distance truck driver, hauling produce and other items up and down the east coast. Aimee Dawn was his right-hand girl, known for riding on the truck or hanging around town with Granddaddy. It was a special treat to "ride out" to Herman's candy store or Tammy and Johnny's Chicken. By age eight, I was on the road, steering the car on Granddaddy's lap then moved on up to driving by myself propped up on a pillow by age nine!

Grandmommy had "sugar" aka diabetes and took insulin shots in the hip every morning. I would sit on the side of the tub in the bathroom while Granddaddy administered her shot because she was too afraid to inject herself. When I turned eight, they started preparing me to give her the shot when Granddaddy was away on the truck. I practiced on an orange from the fruit basket on the kitchen table. I would fill up the syringe with water, aim for and inject the needle into one of those small dots. Even though I practiced all of the time, I wasn't excited about the prospect of actually injecting Grandmommy in her hip and glad I never wound up having to do it, I thought it was gross.

We did the same routine every day. Granddaddy would already be up to do his chores by the time we woke up. Grandmommy would be cooking eggs, bacon, grits, and rolls for breakfast. Aimee and I would get up and go sit down at the kitchen table, bless our food and eat. Since they didn't have a shower in the house, we took a 'wash-up' in the sink. Afterward, I'd get in position in front of the TV to catch "The Price is Right." I secretly hoped a contestant would fall after hearing their name called to '…come on down' or from spinning the "Big Wheel" so hard. I swore, there were a couple of close-calls. If Aimee and I weren't running outside, we would watch 'the stories' with Grandmommy…she loved "As the World Turns," "All My Children," and "Guiding Light."

The house sat on a large-sized plot of land, surrounded by a u-shaped driveway which was littered with broken clamshells, to give the car tires traction. We'd occasionally sit on their front porch, and I became intrigued as I watched them wave at the cars as they passed by. "Who was that?" I questioned. "I don't know," they would reply. It was not a common practice to speak to people I didn't know. However, I learned that it was all a part of southern hospitality. Soon I too got a kick out of "throwing my hand up" at the passers-by.

The large fields were full of cucumbers and other vegetables. In the backyard were a swing set, a clothesline, a wood-framed garage, and an old smokehouse that they used as storage. My favorite chore was to go outside with granddaddy and light the trash on fire. They did not have a trash-collecting service, so, weekly we would take the trash to the backwoods, by the field, and watch Granddaddy strike a match to a piece of paper. He would then stick that paper into a little hole at the bottom of the large barrel until it danced with flames and smoke.

Once night fell, they would 'get the news', watch (Johnny) Carson, then say their prayers. Granddaddy wore a stocking cap, boxer shorts, and a white wife-beater t-shirt to bed every night. One time I found a little bible under his pillow, and he told me that his mother, Grandmother Grace, gave it to him when he was young. I figured

15

she probably knew Jesus because she had already died before I was born. Right before bed, they would each get on their knees to say their prayers. Grandmommy started whispering and wringing her hands, taking deep breaths in between each whisper. I had no idea what she was whispering about so since her eyes were closed, one time I leaned my ear closer to her mouth so I could hear better. The only thing I could catch was, "…and lead us not into temptation." Wait?! Why was Grandmommy praying for The Temptations? I had just seen them, decked out in red bell-bottomed suits, with large afros on the popular music dance show, "Soul Train" hosted by Don Cornelius. Was I not supposed to like their music? Were they bad people? I figured I'd just better not let them lead me either.

Nonetheless, I started copying her…one eye on her to make sure I was doing it right, the other one closed for proper prayer position. I began to wring my hands and whisper, just making it up as I went along. I think I prayed for Mommy, Aimee, our dog Fatima, and for us to be able to go to The Four Corner Plaza the next day to get some Pappy's Pizza.

When we weren't tilling the soil for the next crop of cucumbers on the tractor with Granddaddy, we were helping Grandmommy hang the clothes on the line or mixing the batter for her famous yeast rolls! We knew to walk lightly around the house to allow the yeast to rise before putting it in the oven, and we had a home-cooked meal every day. That was also the place where the sound of crackling thunder and lightning found us sitting with the lights out, in silence, as Grandmommy would say, "Let the Lord do his work." It only took Aimee and me about five minutes before we got separated because we'd be giggling and whispering too much.

The Eastern Shore is where I learned about racism. Coming from the Jersey Shore, as it is affectionately called; I was used to regular beach outings. Once, we asked Granddaddy if we could go to the pool with our neighbors, and he told us, "They don't let little brown babies swim in the pool." Even then, in my seven-year-old heart, I knew that was not right.

There were at the minimum three deaths per summer while we were there, and we did the same routine. The phone would ring, Grandmommy would start screaming and crying uncontrollably then Granddaddy would come to console her, thus beginning the mourning cycle. We'd sit with the family at the house of the deceased, all day long, while people came in and out, bringing their condolences, and other comforts. As a kid, the best part to me was all of the food - fried chicken, macaroni and cheese, yeast rolls, and various types of cakes. We would visit the family each day throughout the entire week leading up to the actual funeral. On the day of the funeral, I always got nervous and anxious when I saw the creepy, black, hearse parked outside of the house. The cars would line up behind the hearse in a procession to the church, it was all very ritualistic and dramatic and scared the crap out of me. There would be a lot of crying, some screaming, and moaning, which scarred me from never wanting to attend funerals if I didn't have to - outside of family members. I managed to skirt the emotional pain of the death of my loved ones because I had never experienced anyone close to me or anyone even dying in New Jersey. As a child on the Eastern Shore, being surrounded by the deaths of my Grandparent's generation, I believed in error that only older people in Virginia died.

I could tell how much we were loved by the way Grandmommy cried every September when it was time for us to go back to New Jersey for school. I vividly remember her standing in the doorway of the porch in her nightgown. Granddaddy holding her up, while she boohooed into a handkerchief. I felt sad that she was crying, but remembered how excited I was to get home to start school. Plus, they didn't have HBO, and the three TV stations signed off at midnight after playing the Star-Spangled Banner, so my TV watching was limited.

My Premonition

In the 5th grade, during a sleepover at my friend Aisha's house, I had a dream in the middle of the night that my Granddaddy was going to die. I woke up startled, sweating, nauseous, and scared. The house was quiet, and everyone was asleep, so I was left to deal with my thoughts and fears, alone, in the dark. Over the next few weeks, I got nervous every time the phone rang at an odd hour. I didn't like for him to be gone on the truck too long. In those days, there were no cell phones so, unless he stopped at a payphone to give us a status update, we didn't know where he was. Occasionally he would call to see if we needed anything from the store before he came home. I pretty much bit my nails the entire time he was away until I heard the loud engines and screeching of the gears shifting announcing he was home and pulling his big truck into the driveway.

A few months after that dream, my Mom was feeding dinner to a bunch of neighborhood children. We were all sitting around the table, laughing, telling jokes, and chowing down when the phone rang. My Mom jumped up to answer it in the kitchen, but for some reason, my stomach automatically dropped, and my underarms started sweating. She closed the sliding door to the kitchen for more privacy. The kids were still laughing, eating, talking, and unaware, but I was utterly dialed into whatever was happening on that phone call. I had no idea what the conversation was about, but my body was beginning to go numb. With that, I slid the door open, walked into the kitchen, made direct eye-contact with her and noting the anxious look on her face, proceeded to throw up all over the kitchen floor. I instinctively knew something was wrong.

Granddaddy had had a massive heart attack in the cab of his truck and was now in ICU, and the prognosis was grim. I knew it! I had never told anyone of my dream but certainly didn't plan to mention it now just in case folks thought I was making it up. I carried that intuitive sense of knowing around with me for many years to come. Granddaddy died the next day, April 27, 1982. He was my first major, personal loss, and I was, we all were, completely devastated.

With the haunting sounds of The Four Tops, "Still Waters" as the soundscape to our somber drive down to Virginia for Granddaddy's funeral, I became keenly aware of how music could make me feel sad. I was afraid to get to the house because I knew the drill. As soon as Grandmommy saw us, I knew she was going to start crying, and the unfamiliar, oppressive grief that remained persistently danced inside of my belly would probably explode on the spot. It all played out just as I'd suspected.

Over the week, we became of recipients of that good ole' southern hospitality, as family and friends came to *our* house with fried chicken, macaroni and cheese, yeast rolls, and various types of cakes. One lady from Grandmommy's church knew my love for vanilla cake with chocolate chip cake frosting and made one just for me. Though I was very appreciative, I didn't want that cake. I just wanted my Granddaddy back. My Granddaddy was the first man I loved that I knew loved me back. On the rare occasions I hear that Smokie Robinson and Frank Wilson penned-song, "Still Waters," I turn the station because even though it has been almost four decades since my Granddaddy 'passed,' I still miss his physical presence.

"Walk with me...take my hand..."

"Still water..."

"Still water..."

"Still waters run deep...still, waters run deeeep"

A year later, one night, while walking down the steps of a neighbor's house, I attempted to bolt down the stairs first to beat Aimee to the car and almost fell. While trying to break my fall, Grandmommy fell off the side of the steps, bruising the side of her ankle. It started as just a small bruise that she and Auntie "dressed" with salves and bandages, but it turned into a full-on medical emergency because over the next few weeks. It went from brown to red to black and full of puss.

Due to her diabetes, Grandmommy's leg was amputated from the knee down because gangrene began eating it away. She eventually got a poorly-designed prosthetic leg but suffered for the most part. It was especially hard coupling the loss of her leg with the recent loss of Granddaddy. Even as a child, I harbored a lot of guilt for that incident because I knew I was the one who caused Grandmommy to fall off of the step that day. Nobody ever outright blamed me, but I knew that had it not been for me, she would still have her leg. She passed away after going into a diabetes-like coma while riding in the car with Auntie in June of 1986. She was only a few yards away from the house she was born in – I consider that a true full-circle moment.

Granddaddy's brother, Uncle George, a WWII Vet and long-distance truck driver, was the King of the Hay Ride…we must have taken one thousand hayrides in his black pick-up truck. Though we drove up and down the same road, he never told us no. He was over six feet, dark, handsome, and soft-spoken. He used to call Grandaddy, "Caledonia", named after the 40's song by Louis Jordan about a woman who had a hard head because she didn't listen. In college, I used to love going to visit Auntie and Uncle George around Labor Day, which was his birthday. I knew my time with them was limited, so I ensured I spent as much time as I could in their presence. I always remember Uncle George would come "peep-in" on me to make sure I was comfortable and that the temperature was just right in the living room where when I slept on the couch. He died a few days after having a stroke in August 1998. Though it was painful, I delivered the eulogy at the funeral.

Ever since I was a child, Auntie and I were tight. One time she even let me say 'shit' without getting into trouble. There were many nights when Uncle George was away on the truck that I got to spend the night at her house. It was easy because Auntie and Uncle George lived in walking distance from Grandmommy and Granddaddy on the same country road. She had the best sense of humor and always had a good one-liner or joke. She was fashion-forward and always sported the latest outfit, purse, or had the newest lamp or kitchen gadget.

One time, we were sitting in the waiting room of a hospital when she lit up a cigarette. She told me that nobody else knew she smoked – supposedly having quit years before. She swore me to secrecy - especially when it came to her sister, Grandmommy. Now she and Grandmommy were inseparable. If they weren't talking on the phone, they were hanging out, but since Auntie was my girl, I wasn't snitchin'. Throughout college and my early 30's, I visited her a few times every year and frequently called her on the phone to catch up.

The day after Thanksgiving 2004, Mommy, my daughter Sydni and I were visiting Auntie at her assisted living facility near Chincoteague, Virginia. We were taking her on a Walmart run for supplies and to get her glasses tightened. As per usual, she got all decked out, full-length mink, blue and gold Chanel scarf wrapped around her neck, and black leather gloves with the leopard fur around the wrists.

On the way out of her room, plastered on the front of her door, was a bright pink piece of paper with the letters DNR (Do not resuscitate) on them. I'd never seen that before or even realized those were her wishes. I asked her about it, but she purposefully ignored my question and went on about her disappointment in not being able to wear her heels to the store. "I want to wear 'them' heels; they just don't want to wear me," she joked about her feet. As we walked into the living room, she talked about getting a new spring coat, as she said, "If she lived and nothing happened." This was a catch-phrase Grandmommy and Auntie were famous for. "I'm going to eat this chicken tonight...if I live, and nothing happens." "I'm going to go to the store next week...if I live and nothing happens." It became a joke to us, so, I was smirking at Mommy as she went on about the potential purchase of this spring coat...but only if she lived and nothing happened.

I escorted her in her walker down the ramp to the car. Mommy opened the car door to help Auntie get inside. "Have you eaten breakfast, Auntie?", Mommy asked. "Huh?", Auntie questioned, looking up into the overcast, gray November sky. Then out of nowhere, she started screaming, "No, no, no!" Still looking into the sky. We all looked up to see where she was looking. I didn't see anything, but she was still screaming, "No, no, no!" We decided to try to sit her into the passenger's seat of my car. So, I ran around to the other side to help guide her in. By that time, she had slumped over and began to throw up the orange juice she'd had for breakfast. Her eyes were closed, and her mouth gaped open into a grimace, baring her teeth. At that moment, I remembered that damn DNR taped to her door.

I was half terrified and half pissed at myself for never committing to taking the CPR classes that were suggested to me once I had Sydni. I figured I could have tried to resuscitate her regardless of what that ole' stupid paper said. She was slumped over in the front seat of the car, and her fingers were turning blue and cold. I started praying and massaging her fingertips, trying to get the circulation flowing again. I was shaking her and holding her in my arms, yelling, "Auntie! Auntie!" Two-year-old, Sydni was in the back, in her car seat pointing at and repeatedly saying, "Mommy, look at Big Auntie!"

Everything became a blur after that. Once I realized there was nothing I could do, I jumped out of the car, screaming and cursing. I had an out-of-body experience. The pain was so immense that I could hear myself screaming, though it didn't feel like it was coming from my actual mouth. I could hear the rocks in the driveway crunching under my feet as I swung at the air, like Muhammed Ali. So much so, that the owner of the assisted living facility asked me to calm down. "How dare she!" I thought. "Doesn't she see Auntie laying there slumped in the car?" I gathered myself and went back in the car to hold the lifeless body of *my* Auntie, *my* girl, the one with whom I had lots of jokes and late-night talks. On our sleepovers, we would lay in double beds, taking bets on the outcomes of the paternity tests on the *Jerry Springer TV Show*, while she smacked loudly on peanuts and talked with her mouth full. It was then that I'd gained a new respect for the term, "If I live and nothing happens..." and vowed to live as much in the present as I could moving forward.

I will never forget or take for granted the foundation that Mommy, Granddaddy, Grandmommy, Auntie, and Uncle George laid for me. I didn't even know that I was learning so much about aging, loss, health, relationships, religion, entrepreneurship, and life through my years spent growing up on the Eastern Shore. From then until now, I've never felt safer than being in between my Granddaddy and Grandmommy, snuggled in their bed.

As I squirmed, tossed, turned, and kicked them in the back while taking up all of the covers, the moon was brightly shining through the window from the field across the street.

Sound Scape: "If I Could" by Regina Belle (Mommy's song for Aimee and me)

Left: Granddaddy, Me, and Grandmommy
Top right: Uncle George, Me, and Auntie at my VSU graduation
Center right: Aimee, Granddaddy, and me on the tractor
Bottom right: Me and Auntie

My Discoveries & Reflections

The Foundation

The Creator could not have selected me for a more loving family because I could not have received any more love, guidance, or support during my early years. During class to become a Certified Integrative Health coach, the instructor asked us to reflect on a time when we felt the safest and the most loved, and to write down who we were with and what we were doing. Nestled in bed between my grandparents is what I instantly envisioned. As the light across the street shone brightly throughout the room, it allowed me to see both Grandmommy and Granddaddy's silhouettes as they slept; I knew nothing could get me because they were on either side of me, protecting me. It was the same feeling I got when I was at home with Mommy's love, safety, and warmth. These are what I call my 'care-free years'. At that point, I'd had no idea what fantastic and frightening experiences lay ahead of me in the future.

I've come to know that we are most in-tune with The Creator when we are children, free from the cares of the world, simply living in the present. As an adult, on the occasion I become scared, anxious or stressed out I've had to remind myself to become child-like again, to quiet my racing mind, and become present and still. I instantly imagine myself, snuggled between Grandmommy and Granddaddy, and those good vibrations of love and safety come flooding back, which allow me to transform those negative feelings into authentic peace.

The Creator placed me in the perfect family on the Eastern Shore because this is where the seeds of topics like aging, entrepreneurship, family, health, nutrition, loss, relationships, and religion were planted in my sub/conscious. Coincidentally, these are the topics I explore most with my private clients in the Goddess Awakening & Healing Sanctuary. I am forever grateful for the foundation that Mommy, Granddaddy, Grandmommy, Auntie, and Uncle George laid for me in my early years.

The Power of Music

Though I didn't understand it as a child, the instruments, frequency, tone, and the lyrics of certain songs can affect your mood both negatively or positively. Music is a powerful healing modality, and whether it is old school hip hop, a Luther gem, or an empowerment anthem, I'm glad I learned early on how to use it to soothe my mind and to encourage my spirit. Whenever I need a little pick-me-up, I know just the right song to put me in a good mood.

Your Reflections
CHAPTER 1

• •

Discuss a time in your life when you felt the happiest, safest, and most fulfilled?

_____

_____

_____

_____

_____

Describe your feelings and emotions about that time in your life. What did it feel like in your body?

_____

_____

_____

_____

_____

wendicherry.com   @AwakenAndHeal

What were you doing? Who were you with?

_____
_____
_____
_____
_____

Do you honestly feel safe, happy, and protected today?

_____
_____
_____
_____
_____

Describe your feelings and emotions about that time in your life.
What did it feel like in your body?

_____
_____
_____
_____
_____

If yes, write about the key experiences that allow you to
currently feel that way.

_____
_____
_____
_____
_____

wendicherry.com   @AwakenAndHeal

If no, ask yourself what are the next *two steps* you can take today to create a better experience for yourself. Sit quietly for a few minutes and allow spirit to give you the answer then write it below.

_____

_____

_____

_____

_____

Play your favorite song. Dance or bob your head, if the spirit hits you! This time, become more present and listen to the song in an entirely new way paying attention to the lyrics, melody, beat. Pick out the instruments if you can.

Write down how it makes you feel, the memories it evokes.

(Ex. When I hear the first few bars of KRS One's "The Bridge is Over", I instantly get excited because it brings back memories of making up dances with my girl Shanay in high school.)

_____

_____

_____

_____

_____

wendicherry.com   @AwakenAndHeal

27

Chapter 2: Dimming My Shine

Shine bright like a diamond! - Rihanna

So, imagine my shock and awe and the fist-full of pearls I clutched when I walked into my third-grade recorder class, and before I could even take my damn seat, this girl whispered that another girl was threatening to kick my ass. "Kick *my* ass?! What did that even mean?", I thought to myself. I looked up at her and naively asked the million-dollar question, "Why?" The answer! …Because *I* thought *I* was cute. Not only did I not understand that concept of "getting my ass kicked," but I also didn't even know the person who was supposed to be administering said ass-kicking. Remember, up until the third grade, I had been living in a bubble…a bubble of love, good vibes, and protection. The day-to-day life with Mommy plus the summers and holidays on the Eastern Shore of Virginia with my grandparents offered me no concept of someone not liking me, let alone threatening to do me bodily harm. Damn!

What I did know was that I was frightened and unsure of my next move. Though I was constantly bullied throughout elementary and middle school, this ass-kicking never actually materialized. There was always the looming threat of someone wanting to "kick my ass." The phrase "Wendi Cherry thinks she's cute" is etched in my mind – still! Not knowing the reasonings for the targeted threats, I only wanted to be friends with everyone. Mostly, I felt a great sense of rejection. I remember telling Mommy, and her only response was, "Well, tell them you are cute!" In my head, I was like, "Yeah, thanks, Mommy, you tryn'a set me up for an ass-whoopin' for real!"

Then there was that time in the 7th grade when I thought I was the black Madonna! Not because I could sing but because I loved her style and music. "Holiday" and "Lucky Star" were my jams! It was the 80's, and I was in full regalia with my lace skirt, headband, and black rubber bracelets – you couldn't tell me shit! There I was, walking on my own personal catwalk going around to the 7th grade homerooms to collect the attendance sheets from each class. As soon as I walked into the last classroom, a wave of laughter erupted that made my heart stop. I looked up to see the majority of the girls, the melanated ones, laughing, teasing, and pointing at my outfit. Embarrassed, I moonwalked my ass right out of there like Michael Jackson on "Motown's 25th Anniversary" special.

In hindsight, that was it! The exact moment where I shut down all of my creativity and started to question my worth. Even though I sewed in high school and have a bachelor's degree in fashion, I always said - out loud - that I was not creative. I used to lie and say that I didn't like dressing up, shopping, or even decorating my home because, in my mind, I didn't have the same skills that my classmates had. That marked the beginning of the many times that I chose to dim my shine. I got used to intentionally walking into a room and playing small.

Unfortunately, this lack of self-worth followed me through my professional career, especially when I was the only woman of color in the room, which sadly was the case on most occasions. I took on the role and burden of being the representative for the entire melanated race when I spoke up, ensuring my voice was heard in meetings. I had no idea how much pressure and responsibility I was placing on my shoulders. As I grew in my professional career, occasionally, I heard that I had a poor and aggressive attitude.

For many years during my reviews, I was passed over for raises, but no one could ever provide a specific instance of me having a bad attitude that…was proven anyway. The so-called accuser's word was always taken over mine without me ever getting the opportunity to address or clarify the issue.

The Fire

Aimee and I grew up having two complete homes, one in New Jersey and the other in Virginia. Mommy decided it was time for us to each have our own rooms so, we converted the playroom into my little piece of pre-teen heaven. I got right to work decorating it complete with a pink canopy bed and a pink princess phone to match, plus a TV, and stereo system. I plastered it with posters from *Right On!* Magazine and my favorite singing group, New Edition.

Unfortunately, in 1985, five days before Christmas, we had a fire in our home that destroyed my entire room. The night before, instead of folding and putting away the clothes that I'd just taken out of the dryer, I put them on the chair next to my bed for later. I placed the old-fashion long wire cable box, on top of the pile of clothes, instead of on top of the TV set where it belonged.

Throughout the night, it had begun to overheat. The next morning, after I'd gotten ready for school, I realized that I'd forgotten my math book. I ran back in, grabbed the book from behind the closet door, and ran out, closing the room door behind me. Thank God for that because the fact that I closed the door saved the entire house from going up in flames. The cable box had gotten too hot sitting on top of that pile of clothes and over the next few hours set the clothes on fire, which quickly spread to the rest of the items in my room – literally turning it into a scorched, black hole.

Later that day, while sitting in class, I heard the announcement over the loudspeaker, "Wendi Cherry, please come down to the office." Huh? Was I in trouble? I thought to myself. Perplexed, I made my way to the school's front office only to find Aimee already sitting in there with the same puzzled look on her face. Our Principal sauntered to sit on the corner of his desk and casually blurted out, "Your house burned down!" My mind raced, and I thought. "What did he just say?" It was all happening so fast; my mind couldn't comprehend what was going on, and I got an instant stomach ache. "Burned down?" I questioned. He suggested that we call our Mom for more answers.

Mommy got on the phone and told us that our neighbor had noticed flames dancing in my room window and thankfully called the fire department. She had been called at work to come home immediately, and by the time she arrived, our entire street was blocked with emergency vehicles. When she got to the house, the fire department had already broken down the front door and had begun throwing my items out onto the front lawn. I gasped then let out a cry because I was in such disbelief. I don't even think my brain was grasping the depths of what had happened. Mommy was angry at the school because she specifically told the Principal and staff *not* to tell us until right before we headed home so we could function throughout the school day.

I was afraid to go home that night and stalled as long as I could, even attending the boys' basketball game, trying to prepare myself for what awaited me at home. After the game ended, I got on the after-school bus and took that long, dark ride home. The bus dropped me at the end of my street, and though it was freezing and dark outside, my armpits were sweating, and my stomach was fluttering. My feet grew bricks as I dragged myself up the long street to my house, at the top of the cul-de-sac. Upon arrival, I could smell the stench of burned matter. Then much to my mortification, I saw the brand-new jeans, the ones I'd just bought with my own money, still smoldering in the grass. The weekend before, I'd gone on a shopping spree in Harlem, New York, and spent my hard-earned money on those cute clothes, all of which were now in a wet, charred pile on the front lawn - I was shocked.

31

When I got in the house, Mommy was sitting at the table with our neighbors. That smell met me at the door, to this day, it is still one of the sickest scents I've ever smelled. Everything in the living room was black with smoke and soot, and the carpet had been water-logged, including the Christmas Tree and the presents under it. When I entered my room, I saw the half-scorched canopy from the bed hanging down onto the mattress, my beloved cassette and stereo set had melted into a pool of metal, all of my favorite New Edition posters had disintegrated in the flames. All of the clothes that had been hanging in the closet were covered in soot, and my christening dress was damaged. Though very devastating, especially only five days before Christmas, we all agreed that we were just grateful that our entire house did not burn down.

My dad and step-mother appeared and showed their support by taking me to JCPenney to buy a few necessities. So, I got the sturdiest types of clothes I could find, Puma sneakers, a pair of jeans, and a few sweaters, which became my wardrobe for the next few weeks. That night, Aimee and I slept over at a neighbor's house because my Mom was afraid someone would try to break in and loot. I had a hard time sleeping all night and kept having nightmares. My neighbor's room window faced directly to my front yard. And because I could not sleep, I woke up at dawn to look out the window only to see Mommy in the cold, in her robe and winter coat, pulling my large, still-smoldering mattress to the curb for the trash truck. Seeing that broke my heart because, at that moment, I wished that she'd had someone to help her navigate this whole process. There she was sleeping alone in a burned house, handling her business just like she always did. I have witnessed her facing many obstacles. For this, I have modeled myself after her strength and tenacity. I am so grateful to her.

The next day at school everybody was asking me questions. The craziest thing was that my basketball coach asked me if my basketball uniform had survived the fire. It pissed me off that he asked about that damn uniform before he asked how my family and I were doing after such a traumatic experience.

For the next few months, Mommy worked with the insurance company to replace my belongings. The pull-out couch in the living room became my temporary bed, but I was anxious to have my own space back. The movie depicting the horrifying story of the Atlanta Child Murders[1], which were a series of murders committed in Atlanta, Georgia, between July 1979 and May 1981, had just come on TV. It highlighted the fact that over those two years, at least 28 children, adolescents, and adults were killed. Though Atlanta was many miles away, most of my peers and I were terrified. My elderly neighbor, Mrs. Johnson, had shared her copy of the *Ebony Magazine*, featuring the photos of each of the deceased children. They looked familiar, just like any other melanated child, I knew.

Claims were made that the murderer was bold enough to enter the homes and bedrooms of some of the children, snatching them right under the noses of their family. Since the couch was right next to the front door, I didn't want to meet the same fate. After a few hours of staring at the front door in pure terror, I began contemplating when I was going to make my mad-dash, past the door, and into Aimee's room for safety. I held my breath, jumped up, and went for it, running past the front door and into her room where she was sleeping. I just tried to hop in the bed with her, but she angrily and sleepily refused. I spent a few minutes pleading my case with her to make room for me in her bed, but alas, she was not having it. Exhausted, I just curled up in a ball, right on the floor, next to her bed, shivering because I had no blanket or pillow, too petrified to go past that front door again to retrieve them.

There were plenty of sleepless nights out on that couch, but thankfully, by April, Mommy made sure my room was whipped into shape. The movie *Purple Rain* by Prince had inspired me to paint it violet. I also got a white daybed, dresser set, and purple violet carpet and curtains. Just like that, I had a brand-new room, everything destroyed was replaced, this was the ultimate upgrade, and I was so grateful for it. Throughout the experience of the fire, the drama it caused, the money spent and finally the restoring of my room, I felt a sense of guilt because the fire was my fault. Had I not put the cable box on the clothes, none of this would have happened.

I'm grateful that Mommy never blamed me, at least out loud. Ha! She always has my back, even in the present, is never judgmental, always encouraging me to try new things, always allowing me to fall and find my way back on my path. There is no way to capture the blessing Mommy is to me. I am eternally grateful that God set it up so that she *Selected ME*!

Daddy Issues

Now my relationship with Mommy was solid, but my Dad, on the other hand, that's an entirely different story. I didn't realize that his absence from my life during my formative years would impact me in the future. I had daddy issues which exacerbated in college because, at some point, my Dad seemed interested in occasionally hanging out with me. I remember the first time he told me he loved me. I was sitting in a chair facing my across-the-hall neighbor's room in Trinkle Hall on the campus of Virginia State University. It was my Sophomore year, and I was wrapping up a rare phone call with my Dad. As I was about to hang up the phone, my Dad said, "I love you." From out of nowhere, birds started chirping, a violin, and harp started playing, and apparently, I was staring into space. Up to that point, I had never, ever heard those words come out of my father's mouth before. I'm not sure what I said next, but we hung up, and I must have continued my random staring. Next, I heard my neighbor, Tonya, calling my name, "Wendi, Wendi, are you ok?" Her question snapped me back to reality. She told me that I'd been staring out into space, so she was just checking on me. I shared the whole story about how my Dad had just told me he loved me for the very first time. I was freaking 19-years-old, so that is a long time not to hear those words from your Dad.

Though it was awkward and a bit embarrassing to share, I was still excited to have heard that vital four-letter-word, L-O-V-E, from my Dad. Throughout my time in college, my dad chose to hang out with me even more! He invited me to bring my friends and Sorors to his home in Chesapeake, Virginia, where we washed our clothes, ate for free, and had a place to crash during the infamous Virginia State vs. Norfolk State football and basketball games. He also gave me money when my car broke down and for other necessities, like the rent for my off-campus housing. When I admitted to him that I wanted to pledge the illustrious Delta Sigma Theta Sorority, Inc., instead of Zeta Phi Beta Sorority, he still agreed to pay my initiation fee. He was a member of Phi Beta Sigma Fraternity, and the Fraternity's Sister Sorority was Zeta Phi Beta Sorority.

One Labor Day weekend, I went to spend time with him at his new apartment in Norfolk, Virginia. We didn't have any specific plans, but I was just happy for the invitation to come to hang out with him. So, imagine my surprise when I walked into the house only to see an attractive young woman sitting with her feet curled up on his couch. She didn't look too much older than me, and I think I noted a smirk on her face. I could hear the washer and dryer swishing in the kitchen and saw an empty laundry basket by her feet. Like Rae Dawn Chong's character Mouse on *The Color Purple* by Alice Walker, I was thinking, "Daddy, who dis woman?"

Uh, you see, my Dad was a married man with a wife living in New Jersey. It seems they'd had some grown-folks agreement to live separately, but I am pretty sure "Lil Miss Feet on the Couch" wasn't a part of that agreement. So, I walked in and introduced myself just as he came out of the backroom. I noted a sheepish grin spread over his face. We exchanged pleasantries and I side-eyed them both because I was curious about what in the hell was going on up in here.

I knew we'd planned to go to dinner at some point during the evening. So, I went to his spare room in the back of the house to put my bags down and to freshen up after a long drive. My Dad had great taste and had the guest room decorated with his Phi Beta Sigma, military, and University of Maryland Eastern Shore (UMES) paraphernalia. Everything was neat and tidy, and I felt comfortable being there. Finally, it looked like he was finally ready to go so, I started making my way to the door. Just then, to my disappointment, he had the nerve to invite her, without consulting me first. I didn't want this lady coming to dinner with us because my intention and hope was to enjoy a rare daddy-daughter dinner. She accepted the invite without hesitation, but as soon as he went into the bathroom, I took it upon myself to uninvite her. I explained to her that I had come to spend time with my Dad...alone. It may have been one of the few times that I had a meal with him by myself. She understood, and when he came out of the bathroom, she graciously told him that she had changed her mind and would call him later. I could tell he was disappointed, but I didn't care; It made me think he didn't want to hang out with me alone, and it hurt my feelings. So, we waited a few more minutes for her to finish folding her clothes, and with that, she picked up her basket and bounced.

Looking back on it, he may have been nervous about spending time alone with me, and she may have been a buffer for him. He was *always* good for a joke and a laugh, but we never had any authentic or in-depth conversations. That wasn't my concern at that point. I mean, hell, he was the adult so he'd have to figure it out.

Admittedly, it was a bit awkward at first but lightened up once the server bought the chips and salsa. We both grabbed a few chips, waiting patiently for the other to dip theirs into the salsa. After crunching on a few mouthfuls, I began trying to fill the dead space. I had it! I'd show him my infamous trick of pulling the straw paper down accordion-style, then putting a drop of water on it while watching it unfurl and move like a caterpillar. He chuckled, and we started talking much about nothing. I still had a nice time and was grateful for a free meal!

Once I graduated from college and moved back to New Jersey, my Dad's calls lessened. We went back to our familiar dance from when I was in grade school to the contact becoming very limited – unless I initiated it. That made my fear of rejection compound because I thought we were beginning to cultivate a cool daddy-daughter relationship. I couldn't help but question myself, trying to understand what I'd done not to make him want to stop engaging. What was it about me that made him not make every effort to maintain our relationship?

As years went on, my Dad's connection with Aimee and me was random and pretty much on his time. We did the obligatory Father's Day, Christmas, and birthday telephone calls, but that was the extent. After his divorce, he reconnected with his University of

Maryland Eastern Shore college sweetheart from the 50's, using the information in the school's alumni directory. They got married in the early 2000's, and instead of an invitation, we got a measly announcement in the mail. It was all good, though. His new wife was nice and did her best to engage in us because, at that point, we were already in our early thirties, so my expectations were low.

Daddy suffered from prostate cancer and was beginning to show signs of early-stage Parkinson's disease. He was swiftly losing his ability to speak, and eventually, it came to the point where he had to stop working as a substitute teacher at the local schools in Princess Anne, Maryland. While his wife worked on UMES's campus, he would go by van to the local adult daycare facility, where he played games and watched TV with the others. He was not the Dad that I remember. Not the loud, boisterous, Leo-man dubbed - Diamond Jim. That guy would walk into the room, announce himself, and buy the whole bar a round of drinks.

It was really sad going to visit him at that place. One time, we took Auntie with us, and though she was older than him, she was in better shape. It was awkward trying to get him to talk and engage, his eyes just looked so lifeless, like he was trapped inside of his body. Once we got back into the car, she just looked at me and said, "Poor fella." We'd all been used to his charisma, and to see him like this was saddening. I heard Mommy mumble under her breath that, "...he'd left a lot of trash on the road." I interpreted it as he'd been so self-absorbed for so many years. Therefore, some of what was happening to him had to be from karma.

That next Father's Day I'd forgotten to call him, and his wife called to reprimand me because he'd started crying. He had limited speech by that point, so phone conversations were tough. I just happened to be at work that day, and it had slipped my mind. Though I was gracious, I had to break that shit down. I shared my 30-plus years' experience with him, and it was evident that he'd told a different story about his involvement in our lives. I wasn't rude. I just figured that she needed a more balanced perspective on our relationship. Just because he was sick didn't change any of the facts that when he was well, he chose not to spend time with me - I was not moved.

Unfortunately, my Dad got bed sores from lying in bed so much. He was rushed to the hospital where he contracted Methicillin-resistant Staphylococcus aureus (**MRSA**), a bacterium that causes infections in different parts of the body and is resistant to some commonly used antibiotics.

He died a few days later after his system completely shut down on December 12, 2007. I was at a Big Daddy Kane concert that night, and when his wife called to tell me he'd passed, for some odd reason, I sat down on the floor and had a little cry, mostly from the shock of it. In reality, I didn't anticipate my life-changing in any obvious way because we'd never been in constant communication, so in my mind, nothing changed.

I did my part and went to the funeral and interacted with family members that I didn't know. All of my life, I'd only gotten to know three of my cousins on his side, from spending a few summers at his sister's house in Chesapeake, Virginia. Kind'a crazy that we could spend time with his sister, but we didn't spend time with him. I remember during the repast looking for a place to sit with my plate. There was one seat left, and I was going to put 5-year-old Sydni on my lap so we could eat. I could hear a woman at the table mumbling about the lack of space. I looked at her and blurted, "It would be nice for Jim's daughter to have a place to sit since it is her father's funeral." The apologies soon followed, but I was ready to roll. It just solidified that I wasn't even recognized by his family as his daughter, which spoke volumes of the lack of connection I had to him.

Honestly, I'd always envied my friends who had relationships with their Dads. I had a great relationship with Granddaddy and Uncle George, but my own Dad was a ghost. I had no idea what it felt like to be a daddy's girl. Those who proclaimed they were daddy's girls always said it with so much pride. I know that studies revealed the importance of the daddy-daughter relationship and the fact that women were prone to energetically attracting men who had the same personality as their father.

I believe my Daddy-wound increased my desire to put so much energy into being a people-pleaser in my romantic relationships. Most of them resulted in me being cheated on, which made me question my self-worth even more. What was it about *her* that was so attractive? What was it about *her* that would cause him to inflict such emotional pain on me, the person he claimed he loved? What *didn't* I have? Was I *not* pretty or *sexy* enough? Why wasn't my dad here to protect me? So, in each consecutive relationship, to make up for that fact, I would effortlessly morph into my partner's world. I ate what he wanted, watched what he wanted, listened to what he wanted, and went where he wanted. I continued that pattern over the next few decades.

Sound Scape: "Shine Bright Like a Diamond" by Rihanna

Daddy and Me (circa 2001)

My Discoveries & Reflections

Daddy

The lack of my dad's presence and interest for the majority of my life led me to seek out male attention and to define my worth by their level of engagement. Though it took me a while, I realized that the reason my dad didn't choose to invest more time in our relationship had absolutely nothing to do with me. He had his shit to work out. Once I accepted that, I felt freer.

YOUR REFLECTIONS
CHAPTER 2

• • • • • • • • • • ● ● ● ● ● ● ● ● ● • • • • • • •

Write about the first time you dimmed your shine. Was it in a personal or professional relationship?

_____

_____

_____

_____

_____

Do you *still* catch yourself dimming your shine in certain situations? YES or NO (circle one)
If yes, write about your experiences. Be sure to distinguish between whether it is in a personal or professional relationship or both.

_____

_____

_____

_____

_____

wendicherry.com   @AwakenAndHeal

Write about why you think you allow yourself to be influenced in this way.

_____

_____

_____

_____

_____

Write about what you will do differently the next time the situation arises.

_____

_____

_____

_____

_____

MANTRA

I AM enough.

I was born perfectly perfect.

Because I was born pure love, there is nothing I need to change about myself to attract the love I deserve.

wendicherry.com   @AwakenAndHeal

Chapter 3: Becoming

"Embrace the pace of your own journey" – Unknown

As an adoptee, I had a strong desire to search for my biological family. The law required that I wait until the age of 18 to request the non-identifying information regarding my adoption. I was grateful for Mommy's support because many adoptees are afraid to tell their adoptive parents that they have a desire to search for their biological families for fear it will hurt their feelings. In my case, I wasn't looking for new parents; I merely wanted to meet the people who had biologically created me. I am grateful that Mommy understood that and helped me start the search for my birth parents on my 18th birthday by helping me write a letter to the New Jersey Division of Youth and Family Services Adoption Division. Five days later, I got a letter from the adoption agency with non-identifying information about my biological parents. (The documents hid the identities of the biological parents preventing either party from contacting without consent). I eventually "found" my birth parents and siblings, who only lived 25 miles north of where I grew up. Additionally, I found an older sister, Erinn, who'd

43

been given up for adoption one year before me, living down south and attending an HBCU in North Carolina.

I soon realized that my birth parents had given Erinn and me up for adoption in secrecy and had vowed never to tell a soul. I couldn't begin to imagine the pain they felt when probably one of their greatest fears was being revealed. It was a great sacrifice to decide to carry, to full-term, a baby that you didn't necessarily plan for and ensure the welfare of said baby by placing them up for adoption. This re-connection caused lots of hurt feelings, confusion, and anger; however, I intended to learn more about myself, never to cause harm. With keeping the information, a secret, there is always a chance said secret could become public – then that's where the shit can hit the fan.

I also believe everything happens for a reason, and I am the one who has the right to choose whether it is a burden or a blessing - it's all about perspective. I choose the latter.

In the winter of 1989, Erinn and I met and bonded instantly. When I heard her sultry-toned voice on our very first call, it sounded like me! We had so many questions for each other...how exciting. Another cool thing is that we were only one year and 11 days apart. She'd grown up "down south" with her mom and two brothers. We put photos of ourselves in the mail immediately! (remember, this was before email and social media). The first time I saw what she looked like, I must have looked at the photo from every angle, looking for similar features - something I'd never seen before. We had a similar skin tone, hair, cheeks, eye, and bone structure. I was so excited! A few weeks later, she came to NJ to visit. I introduced her to every single person in the entire town. We gave each other the nickname, Stis, as in Sister with a 't.'

A few days after my high school graduation, Erinn and I finally got to meet our birth parents for the first time. We'd finally had the chance to speak to our birth mother, who reluctantly agreed to meet us. We counted down the hours and minutes before our agreed-upon meeting time. They'd agreed to come to my house, so, at the appointed time, Erinn and I stood out in the street and the driveway, anxiously waiting for their car to pull up onto the block. That time came and went… A few more hours ticked by, and it was becoming too dark for us to hang out in the street. We both wondered if they were going to show up. Neither of us said it out loud, but I know we were both thinking it and keeping both our fingers and toes crossed that they'd arrive soon.

The June air was pleasant, and all of the windows in the house were open. The genius that I am decided to place my hand-held video camera in my room window to capture every moment of them walking up the long walk-way to the door. However, the lens kept focusing on the window screen versus the long view of the walk-way. Plus, when I made Mommy aware of my plan, she demanded I remove the camera from the window – immediately! My plan was foiled. Undeterred, we came up with the next best thing and secretly placed my small tape recorder inside the potted plant that was in the middle of the living room table. Now, we just had to remember to press play when they arrived…if they ever arrived. We were both getting anxious, and I was beginning to lose hope.

Just then, a big-assed vehicle began to make its way past our house and did an impressive five-point K-turn in the cul-de-sac. It was pretty loud and moving very slowly. We didn't think much of it until said big-assed vehicle parked directly in front of our house. Once it got into the light, we could tell it was a full-sized camper. Could this be them? Erinn and I gave each other the grinch-grin – it was probably just our nervous anticipation. They're here! We ran into my dark room to peep out of the window. I needed to see these people. Who did I look like? I'd always thought I'd probably looked like the mother. I was yelling in my head, "Come on already!" Even though they'd pulled up, they had yet to emerge from the camper.

Mommy turned on the front light, so whoever was in that camper could see better. It was pitch-black out, and the leaves from the trees were hanging down low onto the walkway. It took a few more minutes, but soon a couple emerged, slowly walking up the long walkway from the curb to the front door. I could see the man holding the woman up…she looked terrified. Finally, they walked into the light, and I was able to make out the facial features. I saw her first…I didn't see much resemblance, then looked over at him, and there it was! I could see a few similarities just before they got to the door.

Before they walked into the house, we remembered to press the play button on the tape recorder hidden in the plant. Mommy didn't know about this so, I prayed that we could capture some of our very first conversation for posterity. They came in and took a seat on the sofa. I was staring while trying not to be a creeper. How amazing was this …my birth parents were sitting in my living room?! Mommy helped keep the first part of the conversation on track then excused herself so that we could talk more. Our birth father did the majority of the talking while our birth mother was quietly perusing my photo albums. She looked so nervous and never even touched the glass of water we'd offered her.

Throughout the meeting, we learned that we had four other siblings and that one of them had just gotten married. Overall, the meeting was pleasant, informational, and exciting. Once it ended, there was a promise to reconnect again around the Christmas holiday when we would both be home from college. Though it would take another 23-years for us to have any significant communications, it still ranks among the most exciting moments of my life. …and I still have that tape!

Erinn and I became thick as thieves! We hung out at each other's colleges, hit the ATL for Freak Nik, the Philly Greek Picnic, Virginia Beach Weekend, became connected to each other's friends, were in each other's weddings, and were even pregnant at the same time! At one point, we also lived together and ran two businesses, one a beauty salon, the other an accessories kiosk at a mall in Durham, North Carolina. One time in our apartment during a blizzard, we had cabin fever so badly that every time we looked at each other, we started laughing. I laughed so hard, I could not catch my breath; those were the good ole' days. I was so excited to have an older sister who looked like me, and 30-years later, we are still best friends forever! We have a similar personality, values, sense of humor, and sensibilities. We have supported each other during the lowest of the lows and highest of the highs. Our children, only two-months apart, are now sister-cousins, and we spend as much time together as we can. I couldn't imagine my life without my "Stister"!

VSU

I couldn't wait to get the hell up and out of Tinton Falls, New Jersey, because I never really felt like I fit in. Sure, I had a few trustworthy friends over the years, but in my gut, I knew there was more to explore. Both of my parents and most of my family graduated from a Historically Black College and University (HBCU). Mommy convinced me that I should consider it because of the "polishing" I would get by attending school with staff, faculty, and peers who looked like me.

Admittedly, my grades were average at best, and I got more rejection than admission letters to my college applications. It turns out, my high school guidance counselor was on drugs and on many occasions, directed her melanated students to take the basic college preparatory classes. I was disappointed when I didn't get into my first choice but was still excited to be attending my family's and, more specifically, Mommy's alma mater, Virginia State University (VSU) in Petersburg, Va.

I never forgot her words of wisdom. "Don't rush your college experience. You will never be this care-free again." My pastor, Rev. Andrew L. Foster, Jr., also gave me some sage advice on the day I left for VSU, and that was…"Don't take no wooden nickels from no ni**as!" As soon as he said that, we locked eyes, smirked at each other, then burst out into full laughter. He had a beautiful, deep baritone voice, so his laugh echoed down the block. "I'm serious, Wendi!" he chided. He was like a dad to me, so with that, I promised myself to get involved and fully immerse myself in and take advantage of every opportunity that was unfolding before me.

My very first night at Virginia State University, I wrote the following in my journal:

Date: Sunday, August 13, 1989

Dear Diary,

Well, today was the big day. I am at college in Byrd Hall, room 214. The room is pretty and it's purple. I've hooked it up pretty nicely so far. Now I have to start from the bottom as a freshman. The girl I'm rooming with for band camp is a bitch. Just as long as she is not my actual school roommate, I'm ok.

I pray everything works out with school. Lord, please protect my Mommy.

Wendi

VSU had me at freshman orientation! My new-found-friends and I lived in Byrd Hall. We bonded quickly as we excitedly walked "across the yard," to class, the café, to hang out in front of the student center, Foster Hall, to the football games and plethora of other activities available to us on campus. Having come from a majority European-centered school environment, I loved seeing all of the beautiful and smart melanated people, dressed to kill, handling their business. The hot summer song for 1989 was *"Back To Life"* by Soul II Soul. That joint cranked thru every dorm and car window throughout the first semester of school. Those tight acapella harmonies came first…

"…How ever do you want me?"

"…How ever do you need me?"

Then when the beat dropped, and the claps started…anyone in earshot had to at the very least bob their head. I felt in my spirit that I was home.

I quickly joined the Trojan Explosion Marching Band as a charter member of Silk Phi (the flag squad), The Betterment of Brothers & Sisters (BBS), the Gospel Choir, and Delta Sigma Theta Sorority, Inc. I'd found my place, my voice, my tribe, and my grades reflected it. I made the Dean's list almost every semester throughout college and even had a 4.0 during one semester placing me on the President's List. My good grades plus the recommendation of a professor allowed me to go to the University of Missouri-Columbia

48

for a leadership program for 'minority' students in the summer of 1991.

That said, the one teeny-tiny piece of Mommy's advice that I *did not* follow was not to go to college with a boyfriend. "It's like taking sand to the beach...broaden your horizons," she advised. Now, I'd had the same boyfriend since my junior year of high school, and I was serious. In my naivete, I thought I was going to marry him upon college graduation. I turned my nose up at the new-found attention I was getting from some of the brothers on the yard. I sounded like a back-ground singer for the rapper, Positive K because the only thing that ever came out of my mouth was, "I got a man!" Though I was keenly aware of the plethora of handsome brothas that surrounded me, I only had eyes for him. I made it my business to try to talk to and see my boyfriend as much as possible.

My dorm sisters and I had to take turns using the few payphones located on each of the halls of the dorm. Before the phone even rang twice, it was customary to hear doors fling open and the slide of slippers or flip-flops, scurrying up the hallway to answer it. Fingers crossed it was our man calling us to profess his undying love for us. Chile, please! Wishful thinking, most times, the calls were dramatic arguments where we would hear the desperate pleas of one of our dorm sisters, making her case of why her man should believe she wasn't cheating on him while at VSU.

I can't front, many times that desperate plea was coming from me. It was hard to maintain a long-distance relationship back then. Remember, this was before cell phones, video chat, pagers, and other technology that make our lives so easy now. I made my way up I-95 north as often as possible, yes, to see my boyfriend but to also get a sense of what might be going on behind my back. I'd heard rumors from a few trusted friends that there was some bull shit afoot but was sworn to secrecy not to reveal my sources. This would be the second time; my heart was ripped out of my chest, and my fear of rejection would re-emerge, and my self-esteem would plunge. It was confirmed, the person I considered to be the love of my life, was indeed cheating on me - had been the entire time. I felt so foolish because I'd noticed a few things and asked questions but was always made to feel like everything was a-ok! Why hadn't I trusted my own "women's intuition?" My emotions started swirling, and these questions became my mantra throughout many relationships, for years to come: What was it about *her* that was so attractive? What was it about *her* that would cause him to inflict such emotional pain on me, the person he claimed he loved? What didn't *I* have? Was *I* not pretty or sexy enough?

Saturday Love

As I said, that was the second break-up, my *very first* devastating break-up happened in my Sophomore year of high school. I first laid eyes on *him* three-weeks before my 13th birthday. I was invited by a church friend to my very first co-ed party and was so excited to have been included. I was mesmerized watching these middle and high school kids dancing so closely and seductively (read: bumpin' and grindin'). I was in complete culture shock; I'd never seen anything like that from my peers before. I was half dancing and half keeping my eyes on some of those girls to see if I could bite a few of those moves, but alas, the way my rhythm was set up, that choreography was a no-go. It was all good, because, at that moment, I had bigger fish to fry.

He came out of nowhere, was shorter than me and a great dancer. I didn't have the moves he had, but I was enjoying our dance. *He* had on a white Gilligan's Island-style hat and looked a tad bit like a member of an up-and-coming boy band. I noted that everyone was very casual but hoped he was digging my purple, off-the-shoulder Flash Dance shirt, Jordache jeans, and new purple Kangaroo sneakers that I'd meticulously selected (and stressed over) to attend this birthday party. Just as I was getting my rhythm, the DJ switched up on me and played a slow song. Uh oh, now what? I'd never "slow-dragged" with a boy before! Awhhh, snap, it was my new favorite joint too..."Is This the End?" by New Edition, one of the most popular songs of the time. Without hesitation, he slipped his arms around my waist, and we continued our dance.

A kaleidoscope of butterflies came to flutter directly in my belly. I breathed deeply, trying to suppress the smirk that was slowly unfolding across my lips like a Cheshire Cat, and quietly counted one…two…one…two, doing my best to keep up with his rhythm. I started to sweat, keeping my face to the side to avoid direct eye-contact. On the inside, my heart was racing. Who was this guy? I had never seen him before but was immediately smitten. I snapped out of it once the song ended, and he disappeared into the crowd. I didn't know many people from the party, so I didn't have anyone to help me I.D. him; though a few weeks later, my church friend told me that he'd asked about me! As fate would have it, an entire two-years passed before I reencountered him but the details of that night – that song, my off-the-shoulder Flash Dance shirt, the venue, his energy, all remain etched in my heart and mind to this day.

We officially began dating my freshman and his junior year of high school. Everything around us was influenced by hip hop. It was such an exciting time, and it didn't hurt my credibility to have a boyfriend, who was funny and could beatbox *and* dance *and* looked cute in his blue shearling jacket and shell-toed Adidas with the fat laces. He was my man, and I was his girl, and though we didn't drive yet, we relied on our left and right feet to walk to each other's houses to spend as much time as we could together. I almost died when I got grounded for having a 'D' in Spanish class.

My mom was not playing and kept me on punishment for the entire marking period until I brought that grade back up. So, our theme song became "Saturday Love" by Cherelle and Alexander O'Neal because we could only see each other on the weekends.

"Sunday, Monday, Tuesday, Wednesday, Thursday, Friday, Saturdaaay love…"

"Sunday, Monday, Tuesday, Wednesday, Thursday, Friday, Saturdaaay love…"

In the beginning, it was easy-breezy, fun-loving, and innocent. As time went along, though he never directly pressured me with sex, I still got the sense it was always on his radar, and I was petrified. My good group of girlfriends, affectionately dubbed, 'Fly Girls Only,' aka FGOs, was in the class of 1987, and I, the baby of the group, was set to graduate in 1989. These girls were much more sophisticated and experienced in the real world than I was. One night during one of our sleepovers, they were having a very intimate, vulnerable, and sobering talk about sex, sharing their experiences with the guys who had treated them differently afterward. I was clinging to and trusted every word they said, and when it came to my turn, I didn't have a story to tell. They seemed relieved by that and swore me never to have sex with anybody, especially if I was not ready. Those words became etched in my mind but didn't bother me much since I was considered what some would call a "good church girl." These girls were crying about the pain, and I wanted no parts of it. So, I almost wore a "good church girl" as a badge of honor.

Our relationship lasted for less than one year, but to me, it was everything. Inevitably the time came when the calls and visits started to dwindle. So, I did the things that I thought would get his attention. On a trip to see my God-Sister, Jordan, at Howard University in Washington, D.C., I cut my hair in the latest, asymmetrical-style with flat-ironed crimps, just knowing that would get him back. I also bought a few cute outfits that I thought he would like. In the end, it was hard to keep his gaze because he was already on to the next one. One night he called and very matter-of-factly told me he was 'quitting me.' I started crying, and in the coldest voice, he spat, "Stop crying!" At that moment, I remember gazing into my own eyes while standing in the bathroom mirror and choking down and swallowing that cry, hard, in the middle of my throat. That was the first time; I'd considered those damn questions. What was it about *her* that was so attractive? What was it about *her* that would cause him to inflict such pain on me, the person he claimed he loved? What didn't *I* have? Though I have never bothered to confirm this, a little birdie told me it was because I wouldn't sleep with him. I unknowingly carried that memory of rejection deep within my heart and spirit, like a bag lady, for years to come.

Stinker and Princess

The next eye-opening and heart-wrenching, romantic experience I had begun one chilly September night at the small corner store at the edge of Virginia State University's campus. I called myself sneaking into the store to buy a perm for my hair so, I threw on some sweat pants, a jacket, and a hat. The store was empty besides the cashier and lo-and-behold *HE* walked in, and as soon as we locked eyes, he flashed that infectious grin. We had recently seen each other on the yard but had never had a conversation. He made a bee-line for me and asked me what I was buying. I was a little shaken because I knew I looked crazy. I hadn't expected to run into anyone, especially *him*. I told him I was buying a perm, and he asked if he could take off my hat, which I allowed because I was intrigued by this gesture. He felt my tangled ponytail and announced that, in his opinion, I shouldn't be putting any chemicals in my pretty hair. I told him I wouldn't buy it if he would come over every day to tame it for me. We joked a bit more, and he finally asked if he could have my phone number.

From that night on, we became inseparable. He was my 'Stinker,' and I was his 'Princess.' I was spellbound and within a few months, we became next-door neighbors and spent all of our nights together. We had many highs and lows throughout what was my last year in school. Sometimes we'd hang at his house, other times we'd hang at mine. We got tight and selected Chante Moore's hit, "Love's Taken Over" and "Weak" by SWV as *our* songs. There was also the slamming of doors after a heated argument. Periods of no communication. Loud guffaws as we cooked our favorite chicken wings, collard greens, baked beans dish, and hours-long, intimate, heart-opening talks about our dream of getting married. We saw each other every day, on and off-campus. As relationships do, this one started so sweetly, but that sugar turned to shit very quickly.

What was supposed to be a festive and celebratory occasion turned into my nightmare. All of this occurred, on the night before my graduation ceremony, that was being held on Mother's Day. My family had just come into town, and everybody was partying. My roomies and I were having a graduation celebration at our house, and we were all having a ball. Just then, I noticed that my boyfriend wasn't there, and since he lived right next door, he had no excuse not to be. So, I dipped-out right quick and ran next-door to see where he was. I found him, laying crossed-legged on his bed, watching T.V., giving off that very familiar, stank-assed energy.

Something felt off so, I took a deep breath and asked him what was wrong. He didn't want to talk about it and refused to answer my direct question. I thought it was odd but wasn't in the mood for his foolishness, especially the night before my graduation. So, I made an about-face to head back thru the kitchen, out the back door, and across the grass to finish partying with my friends and family. As soon as I pushed the door open, he came to the kitchen and spat, "You could have at least told me you were inviting your ex-boyfriend!" Having no idea what this man was talking about, I stood there stunned. "What ex-boyfriend?" I questioned. Of course, no ex-boyfriend of mine was there, and I wasn't in the mood to argue about it. So, as I was attempting to open the door, he jumped in front of me and slammed it shut. WTF?! The look in his eyes was menacing. Usually, he was a gorgeous, nicely-built, curly-haired chocolate-drop with an infectious gap-toothed smile. But, honey, not today, that smile turned into a sneer, and this mean streak, that I had seen before, was in full-effect and flashing through his eyes.

I could hear his two other roommates in the house, so I was trying to be cool and keep whatever this was, quiet and controlled. I intended to try to make him understand that everything was cool, that he had nothing to worry about because I would have never invited an 'ex' to my graduation. Was he losing it? I had no idea where he even conjured up such an idea. Before I knew it, he was pushing me back through the kitchen and into his bedroom where he slammed the door behind us.

Yo, I felt like I was smack-dab in the middle of The Twilight Zone because whatever story he had been telling himself, in his mind, was straight facts. He was not letting this issue go or letting me leave the house. He knew my people were next door. Then I began to worry because I just remembered that I hadn't even told anyone I was leaving. I'd intended to run over, grab him and get back to the party.

I did not know why he was doing all of this, but honestly, this was not a new occurrence. He very frequently would go off, conjuring up crazy accusations, off-the-wall stories, but not tonight, I was so not in the mood for his shit. All I wanted was my boyfriend to come next-door and join the celebration with the rest of my friends and family. So, I very delicately asked him to explain to me exactly why he was so upset. This just seemed to exacerbate the situation. "You think I'm stupid, don't you?" he sneered. "Why you tryn'a play me out?"

In such disbelief, I began to tune him out and noticed on the wall, the brand-new picture of a cute, little chocolate-colored girl with locs and big, beautiful, brown eyes, hauntingly staring back at me. I'd loved this print and had recently given it to him as a gift from a local African store. He, too, loved her unique image, so when we hung her up on his wall, we decided to name her Stormy. So, there was ole' Stormy, staring at me and what I'd always remembered as beautiful eyes now somehow looked sad. It seemed like we were having a staring contest, and in my mind, she was asking me how in the hell I'd gotten here? Her non-verbal response was everything. At that moment, I felt as sad as she looked. I began reminiscing on how just a few days prior, we'd shared such a beautiful moment, selecting the perfect place for her on his wall. Right then, noticing that I was staring at Stormy, he ripped her down, tearing her to shreds, which he proceeded to throw in my face. He knew that would trigger me because I'd been so happy to give him that print. My clap-back, Scorpio energy, would not allow me to be outdone! I'd been known to match a little crazy with crazier in my time so, I picked up his lamp and threw it, as hard as I could, across the room and watched it slide down the wall into little pieces.

Oh, shit! It was dark in there now so, it was on and poppin'. He proceeded to throw the full champagne flute that was sitting on his nightstand, into my newly-coiffed and colored graduation, Halle Berry-esque hair. Damnit! I just paid good money to get my hair done, and I was pissed. Totally over it, I tried to escape, running back through the kitchen out of the back door, across the yard back into my house, where I could get some help. Easier said than done. As I tried to run back to the kitchen, he grabbed me again. One of his roommates, hearing the ruckus, peered out and asked if everything was ok. "Man, what are you doing?" his roommate questioned. The roommate was looking at me with such pity but at my boyfriend with fear, so I still didn't feel safe. He told him to shut up, mind his business, and flinched at him with his fist. With that, his roommate retreated into his room, giving me a sad and worried look. This particular roommate had been my friend long before I even met my boyfriend, but I could tell he did not want to get involved.

Relentless, I kept making my way towards the door where he surprisingly opened it and pushed me out but not before ripping my t-shirt off, exposing my bare breasts into the dark, steamy, May night. Luckily for me, nobody was outside. So, I quickly covered myself and started running for dear life across his backyard and into my driveway. I'd just realized that I had my house and car keys in my pocket, so I began fumbling, trying to get my house key ready to bust that front door wide open. Using his football skills, he bolted out of the door, right behind me so, I hastily went for the car instead. I scrambled with the keys a bit but got the car door unlocked and jumped in to lock it before he could get me. Unfortunately, he jumped in right before I could get it locked it and I wound up locking us *both* in the damn car. Shit! "What now?" I thought.

Inside the car, he continued his tirade of crazy accusations. Exhausted, I began beeping the car horn furiously, praying that somebody would hear the commotion and come outside to help me. Finally, one of my roommates came to the door, and I kicked that car door open, like Jackie Chan, and ran like hell through the front door – topless. You can imagine the stares that I got as I ran into the house. Everybody was looking at me crazy because the last time they had seen me, we were happily cutting our graduation cake. No one had a clue as to what had just transpired over the last 30-minutes. I ran upstairs to my bedroom to get dressed and began to tell the story. Everyone's mouth was gaped open, and I still felt like it had all been just a dream. My sister suggested I call the police. For some reason, in my crazy mind, I was a little hesitant, so somebody did it for me. I grabbed the phone and hung it up. Immediately, the police called back, telling us that it was a requirement that they send a patrol car to check out the scene. I refused to bring any charges or even to tell them the story. He eventually came over, even more infuriated, yelling, "Oh, so, you want to call the cops on me now?" Uh, not really, I only just wanted to enjoy my graduation night with peace and calm, and fun. I had no idea why and how this night took such a horrible turn. How could he do this to me on my special night?

The rest of the night was a complete blur, but I do remember everyone keeping an extra eye on me. He stayed at his house, and I stayed at mine. Graduation morning, I woke up late, exhausted emotionally, spiritually, and physically. My roommates had to leave ahead of me since our call-time was just a few minutes away. I seriously could not pull myself together - my once beautiful hair was now crunchy and destroyed due to the champagne toss from the night before. Heart beating a mile-a-minute, I managed a shower, slipped on my cute lil cream and brown, striped GAP dress, brown suede platform heels, and dashed out of the door, with my cap and gown. I didn't have an appetite, so I never attempted to eat before trekking out into this long, hot-assed day. I made my way on the yard and into my place in line, right before the whole class began processing into the stadium. Ugh, it was so hot, and I was so nauseous. I couldn't get my shit together. I just kept replaying the night's events over and over again in my head. What in the hell was wrong with him?

The class of 1993, marched through the gravel to the graduation stage, where I was finally able to sit down. These new platform shoes were cute but hard to walk in on all of this gravel. My left shoe was already rubbing against my bunion. It was so uncomfortable sitting in the direct sun with that black, polyester robe on - I was miserable. I'd never even made contact with Mommy, Auntie, Uncle George, Aimee, and my bestie Fern that morning before graduation. I wondered if Aimee or Fern had told Mommy what had happened the night before. I was a lifeless, emotionless body, going through the motions on what should have been one of the biggest celebrations of my life.

I could not pay attention to the graduation speeches or performances because my mind was replaying the scenario from the night before. It was more horrible than I'd even remembered. The details were crystallizing in my mind, and yo, it was frightening. At some point, I felt like I would pass out. I had what they called 'vasovagal syncope' response [2], since age five.

Vasovagal Syncope Response happens when your body is overheated, in fear, traumatized, or from standing too long, etc. The body shuts down to protect you. It had happened to me on many occasions before so, I could feel it coming on. I didn't want to let on to the people sitting to the left and right of me that I wasn't feeling well, but I almost didn't have a choice. I unzipped that hot-assed black graduation gown and tried to get more air. I was fanning myself with my program, trying to fight back that familiar salty taste I would get in my mouth right before I was about to go down. Like an angel, someone tapped me on my shoulder and handed me what looked like a mirage. From up in the stands, Mommy, who knew her daughter so well, could tell I was struggling. So, in her quick thinking, got me a large cup of Sprite and found a way to pass it down the bleachers, through all of the graduates. Talk about a miracle; I was pretty close to the front of the stage in the "C" group. That was truly divine intervention that my mom had found me, sensed what was going on, from way up in the bleachers, and was able to send me that Sprite. I gulped that entire cup down like I'd been in the Mojave Desert for the last hour.

Thank God because I needed to feel better in time for my row to make our way, one by one, across the stage. I'd kept on my black sunglasses because I probably looked as fatigued as I was feeling. "Wendiii…Cherrry!", said the MC from the loudspeaker. Finally, it was my time, so my wobbly brown platform shoes, and I made our way to shake the hands of the dignitaries handing out the degrees. I turned to look and wave at the crowd and mustered up the best fake smile that I could. Unbeknownst to anyone else, I'd practiced and planned to do a little dance upon receiving my degree, but alas, due to the circumstances, I didn't have it in me so, I just got grabbed my 'piece of paper' and kept it moving.

This was far from the graduation celebration I'd envisioned. As I made my way down the stairs to begin the walk back to my seat, over all of the yelling, cheering and talking, I heard a familiar voice yell out, "I love you, Princess!" I looked up, and there he was with that heart-melting, sneaky, gap-toothed grin. Admittedly seeing that curly-haired joker standing there made my heart flutter, and I yelled back, "I love you too!" and damn-near floated back to my seat. Having him there, after all, we'd been through the night before still had to count for something…riiight?! I joined my line sisters on "the block" in front of Virginia Hall to do our famous Delta traditional 'circle songs.' My feet were killing me, the sun was even hotter, but this was one of those moments I'd lived for since freshman year – to sing along with my Sorors and celebrate each other's accomplishments. He was lurking in the shadows over by the trees, grinning at me from a distance. I knew there was a larger issue I needed to contend with deep in my heart. I had just enough energy to finish the songs and make it back to my house.

After graduation was over, my whole family came back to our filthy Greenwood Drive house in Ettrick, Virginia. I was so embarrassed. With all of the partying the night before, nobody had taken the time to clean up. Click! Click! It took everything in me to stand there and smile for the camera, but I knew how important this day was, and I was grateful that everyone was there to share it with me. I made it a priority to reenact a picture that Mommy had taken with her Grandmother Grace on her college graduation day with Auntie and Uncle George.

Once they were gone, like an inchworm, I crawled on my belly, up the stairs to my bedroom and just laid there, lifeless. I did not have a single ounce of energy left. It was hot outside, and we didn't have any air-conditioning, so my room was sweltering and a complete mess. The house was quiet because everyone else had gone out to eat with their families. So, I just laid there on the floor, still in my graduation dress, trying to muster up enough energy to go back downstairs to get a glass of water. I got down the stairs only to remember there were no clean dishes. So, I filled up a plastic measuring cup and went back upstairs, praying to sleep for the next week. In my heart of hearts, I was still hoping this was all a nightmare, and I would awaken soon.

Ughhh! Thirty minutes had passed and between the stifling heat and that one damn fly, that kept buzzing in my ear-tickling my stomach, I still hadn't gotten any sleep. So, you can imagine my vexation when the phone started ringing. Since no one else was home, I had to get up again and answer it. "Hello?" My heart skipped a beat when I recognized *his* voice on the other line. "Are you ok?" he questioned. "I am so sorry about what happened last night.", he said in a gentle voice. "Come over, and I'll take care of you." Before I knew it - without knocking - he burst through the front door, stomping up the stairs to my room, yelling out his pet name for me, "Princess...Princess!" "Damn! It's hot up in here", he said once he got to the top of the stairs and saw my fully-dressed, motionless body lying on the floor. With that, he scooped me up and carried me back down the stairs and across our adjoining yards to his house. He then put me in his bed and let me sleep for hours. He periodically woke me up to give me water and even made me eat a big bowl of SpaghettiO's because I hadn't eaten since the party the night before.

It was midnight by the time I woke up to find him quietly lying there just watching the T.V. and me. He caressed my hair, one of his favorite things to do, and encouraged me to go back to sleep, which I did without hesitation. The next day, I was supposed to start packing up my entire college existence and make my way back to New Jersey. Honestly, I didn't have a job to go home to, so I planned to hang out down at VSU and play house for the summer. I wasn't ready to get a "real job." Mommy's mothering instinct must have sensed the B.S. because she called and told me I needed to start making my way home - sooner rather than later. Then to top it off, Auntie called promising me some lobster tails and crabs if I would come home ASAP. What a trap! They had me at lobster tails. I knew it was time to go, so, over the next week, I reluctantly packed and slowly drove my way up I-95 north and into the real world.

I am embarrassed to say that the summer and fall of 1993 continued to be just as emotionally draining as our college days. I was constantly driving between VSU, his hometown, and trying to get a job, which I finally landed in Harlem, New York. I was so excited to be working at The World-Famous Apollo Theater on the *Apollo Comedy Hour* T.V. show in the wardrobe department.

My first real job and I was putting my college degree to good use. It was fast-paced and exciting, except it was unpaid. So, I juggled a few other money-making jobs, including taking on the one of ensuring he knew he was an important part of my life. He was a "super senior" now and still had one more year to play VSU football. I could tell he was a little jealous of me, and on our daily calls constantly nagged me about meeting other people in New York.

By winter, again, things were getting out of control. He was back to being accusatory and mean on the phone. I was confused and doing whatever I could in my power to make him understand that I only had eyes for him. It was true; I wasn't remotely interested in anyone else. He came to visit for Christmas and even joined me in the hospital to welcome my first-born, niece Amee'ra into the world. He was acting odd, but at that point, I was used to it and less inclined to try to figure out his issues. He spent a few more days with me then headed off to what I now know was his other girlfriend's house...yep, you read that right, his *other* girlfriend's house, which was 30 minutes north of my home in New Jersey.

Over time it was revealed that he'd had this new girlfriend since the summer when she became a freshman at Virginia State University. So, the entire time I'd been stressing myself, trying to include him on all of my daily activities, he was cultivating a relationship with another young woman. I also came to learn that during all of my visits, she had just been hidden out of sight until I left so that they could return to their normally scheduled programming. I was the "Wife," she was the "Boo-Boo." Once I called him on it, he tried to blame her. But at that point, I was smart enough to know that it was all on him; he was the only one who made me all these promises to love me forever. He was the one who told me that we were going to get married. He was the one who said when his football career took off; we were going to move and enjoy a beautiful life together. On the real, repeating some of the stories makes me feel so stupid and reminds me of how naïve I was back then, but I am hoping that this experience will inspire someone else to not fall for the okie-doke.

The most heartbreaking part was that he'd gotten her pregnant. That was the lowest blow because he'd assured me that I was his only sexual partner...I know, I know... duh, Wendi! That was a blow that I would not recover from for many years. As soon as I would come home from work, I would bury my sorrows in Vanilla Crunch ice cream and chocolate chip cookies. Slowly but surely, I stopped talking to him completely and finally went on with my life. I had gotten a job with MTV as a "Roadie" on their United States spring break college tour. I was so excited because I loved to travel. Our job was to set up marketing campaigns – getting college students to sign up for credit cards for a t-shirt. Unfortunately, I was the one hawking the credit cards. The money was good, we ate out every night and got to see the changing landscapes of the east coast and southwest parts of the country while driving from campus to campus.

It was 1994, and Mary J. Blige had just dropped her famous, *My Life* album. We just happened to be on the campus of Clemson University in South Carolina, and I scoured every record store to find my copy. Once I copped my compact disc (CD), I devoured every single word of every single song in the liner notes while sitting in the laundry mat. My new Sony Walkman earphones hugged my ears, and every instrument, note, and beat struck a chord in my heart and soul like never before. I didn't have anybody to co-sign the dopeness of MJB with me since I was the only melanated woman on tour, and the other Roadies liked rock 'n' roll and country. It was all good, because from my very first listen, my favorite song on the album became, "Be Happy."

Mary's question was so deep but yet so basic,

"How can I love somebody else..."

"If I can't love myself enough to know..."

"When it's time, time to let go-o-o-o?"

There I was, all alone. Sitting on top of the washing machine, with that song on repeat, and tears streaming down my face. Me too, Mary, me too! I repeated to myself. It was a question I would come to ask myself for years to come. It didn't feel like too much to ask. I only wanted to be happy and to find that special kind of authentic love that could stand the test of time.

He and I hadn't spoken regularly for a few months, but the MTV folks asked for suggestions for additional people for the tour because it was creating a new west coast route. I was a part of the east coast tour and thought he might do well as a west coast "Roadie." He'd graduated by then and still didn't have a job, so since he owed me a significant amount of money, I figured this was a good way for him to pay me back.

He was hired immediately and headed out west while I stayed east, but we started to talk more commiserating our experiences of being the only melanated people on tour. By March 1995, the east and west tours merged and headed to South Padre Island at the very tip of Texas right on the Mexican border. We set up shop there for the next month, while drunken white college kids came to wreak havoc on the island for their spring break. We were all given a fully-furnished beach home plus our choice of roommates. Up to that point, I hadn't physically seen him since Christmas 1993 so, I wasn't sure what to expect.

He appeared to be very grateful that I'd suggested him for the job and happy that he got to make some money and travel. He promised that after the tour, even though we still weren't together, he would make good on his college promise to take me to Disney World. I'd already bonded with a girl named Christina from Texas, who didn't mind if he roomed with us. So, the three of us set up a home in a cute little beach house complete with a deck that jutted right out into the Gulf of Mexico. We would work on the beach all day and party around town all night. It all started out nice enough but declined very quickly. I'd met other people on tour and had been talking to them via payphones, and he'd seen messages come up on my SkyPager. It didn't take long for us to fall back into our old ways of him always being accusatory and angry and me trying to figure out what to do to make him feel better. I was embarrassed for both of us at this point because we were the only melanated roadies, and I did not want them to see us acting unprofessionally. As our roommate, Christina knew what was happening but was so compassionate and fair towards both of us; she never told anybody else what was taking place and on a few rare occasions, acted as the mediator between us.

I wished I'd never invited him to join this tour company. My travel experience was now being affected by his energy. He was like Dr. Jekyll and Mr. Hyde, one day he was the sweetest, funniest, most understanding and kind man I knew then the other times, I had no description. The month dragged on, and I'd gotten food poisoning a couple of times - the last one was so bad that I was rushed to a hospital in Matamoros, Mexico, where I got a bad needle stick when they attempted to administer some pain medicine. This created nerve damage in my hip, which impacted my ability to feel anything for a few years afterward. He decided to switch to the east coast side of the tour so that he could help take care of me and so that we could be together, but I quickly realized that was a bad idea and quit the tour while he stayed on.

I seriously needed to take the freakin' hint and move on with my life so, I moved to Durham, NC, to live with my older sister for a change of scenery. Right before my move, he made good on his promise and took me to Disney World. We had the most magical time of our entire three-year relationship. I mean, you really can't act the ass with the enchanted energy of Mickey and Minnie Mouse all around you. We were away from the stressors of everyone and everything that we knew, and it was delightful. Our room was perfect, we dined in beautiful restaurants, rode the rides, and took lots of pictures, even getting the Disney characters to sign our autograph book.

During that trip, I got to see him in his most authentic, innocent, and child-like self. Overall, we just enjoyed each other, and now that he has passed into the ancestral realm, it is one of the fondest memories I have of us. I'm so grateful we got to make our peace during the CIAA Tournament in Charlotte, NC, a few years before he tragically and unexpectedly passed away. To this day, every time I hear our songs, "Love's Taken Over" or "Weak," I can see his sly grin and get a good chuckle of all of the crap we both encountered. Though it took years, I came to understand that his behavior was just a culmination of all of the hurts and pains that he'd experienced over the years. Honestly, he was just being him, but the real question was, what was within me that would allow me first to attract such a person and secondly put up with such poor treatment for so long?

I began asking myself…

Why I was so invested in making him love me versus me loving myself?

Why was I committed to staying in an unhealthy and volatile relationship?

I surmised it was my fear of rejection. I only wanted to be loved, and because we were so explosive, in my crazy mind, it made me feel like the drama meant it was something real. This was not rational, and I knew that I deserved to be in a better relationship than that.

Overall, my beloved Virginia State University ranks as one of the best experiences of my life. I met some of the most wonderful people and created bonds and friendships that have grown even stronger over the last 30-years. My HBCU experience exposed me to different types of people, opportunities, experiences, and situations. Those years were the very beginning stages of my evolution, where I came into myself – was becoming a woman, and for this, I am eternally grateful.

Sound Scape: "How Ever Do You Want Me" by Soul II Soul

Freshmen year in front of Virginia Hall at Virginia State University, 1989 (Photo: Tadpole)

My Discoveries & Reflections

Identity

In the case of my adoption search, I am now clear that knowledge of self is a birthright, and I never needed anyone's permission to explore my biological roots or any other part of me. It is also important because as health issues arise, a complete transfer of genetic health history data could save an adoptees' life. It is evident with the increased interest in DNA testing companies that humans yearn to learn more about themselves intimately, and I wholeheartedly support anyone wanting to know more about their genetic roots.

Rejection

Though as an adopted child, I developed a strong bond and felt safe within the foundation that my Mommy and extended family created for me, unconsciously, I still felt the unrelenting nagging of the fear of rejection. It wasn't until my late 40's that I learned the energetic effects that being rejected at birth had imprinted in my DNA. I have learned that trauma begins in the womb. The lack of bonding between a fetus and its birth mother affects the baby into adulthood.

In my case, I was given up for adoption in secrecy, which means, my birth mother never intended to bond with me.

Normally a very outgoing and happy-go-lucky young woman, I would easily descend into an emotional wreck after my relationships ended. Of course, everyone remembers their first heart-break or traumatic experience with someone they love. Still, for years, I couldn't understand why I couldn't simply shake those bad feelings and move on, especially in relationships where the other person didn't have my best interest at heart.

According to marriage and family therapist, John Amodeo, PhD[3]:

"The fear of rejection is one of our deepest human fears. We are biologically wired with a longing to belong, we fear being seen in a critical way. Unconsciously, we may be afraid that rejection confirms our worst fear — perhaps that we're unlovable, or that we're destined to be alone, or that we have little worth or value."

The article, "I Adopted My Child at Birth What Do You Mean Trauma?" gave me more insight into why the fear of rejection had haunted me so unforgivingly all of my life. Author Alex Stavros, President and CEO, Calo Family of Programs[4], along with contributing authors, provided insight on this topic.

Below are a few excerpts from adoption-related articles that have impacted me and helped me on my healing journey.

- Even in the most loving and supportive adoptive homes, it is in and of itself a form of trauma. Without the biological connection to their mother, even newborns can feel that something is wrong and can be difficult to soothe as a result.

- Babies began feeling and learning in the womb. According to Samuel Lopez De Victoria, Ph.D., a baby learns to be comforted by the voice and heartbeat of its mother well before birth[5]. In the case of adoption, this connective disruption has an impact on the brain and body.

- Surprisingly, babies are also able to sense a disconnection or lack of acceptance from their mother while in the womb – leading to attachment issues and developmental trauma down the road.

- Mothers that end up placing their child with adoptive parents are also likely to feel increased stress during their pregnancies. Each of these stressors could expose unborn babies to cortisol, leading to stress. The baby is then born anxious, which can impact the sense of safety and self-worth for the child. Critical brain development is also stunted.

- An infant with a stressed mother has more difficulty regulating and managing their stress reactions later in life. Babies can be born with a predisposition to diabetes, depression, anxiety, PTSD, and addictive behaviors simply because of the environmental factors of the mother's womb.

One of my favorite Institute of Integrative Nutrition, professors and well-known obstetrician, Dr. Christiane Northrup discussed in her 2005 book, "*Mother-Daughter Wisdom*" [6], the science behind the familial bonds that shape our physical, mental, and spiritual well-being.

- Dr. Northrup shares that if a pregnant mother is going through high levels of fear or anxiety she creates a "metabolic cascade." Hormones known as cytokines are produced, and the mother's immune system is affected, along with her child's. Chronic anxiety in the mother can set the stage for a whole array of trauma-based results such as prematurity, complications of birth, death, and miscarriage.

- The mother-daughter relationship sets the stage for our state of health and well-being for our entire lives. Because our mothers are our first and most powerful female role models, our most deeply ingrained beliefs about ourselves as women come from them. Dr. Northrup notes that our behavior in relationships—with food, our children, our mates, and ourselves—is a reflection of those beliefs.

I was astonished. How come I'd never heard of this theory before? I had no real connection to anyone along my biological mother's ancestral line because of being adopted at birth. I'd only heard names, and I did not know anything about their personalities, life, and childhood experiences or traumas. I just knew that as an adoptee, I was raised in a happy family. Nature vs. nurture was at play here.

Discovering this information has been critical on my journey to awakening and healing myself, which in turn will have a ripple effect on my child and family. I was able to make the connection between my lack of self-esteem and poor decision-making process. I used to think that had I been exposed to this information earlier, my life would have turned out differently but understand that it came when I was ready to receive it. I don't think that I would have been able to absorb it and distill it the way that I can now.

To clarify, this also happens in the lives of children who were *not* put up for adoption. Each of our beliefs was ingrained into us regardless of our birth mothers were over the moon, excited to be carrying us or were utterly stressed out about being pregnant. Though not a clinical diagnosis, there is a phenomenon called "the mother wound." According to spiritual advisor, Suzanne Heyn[7], common emotions related to the mother wound include feelings of being fundamentally flawed, not good enough, not deserving of your dreams, or like you have to stay small to maintain the affection of others. If you have difficulty setting boundaries or feel like you need to take care of everyone around you, then you probably have wounds in this area.

This information should not be used to play the blame game but to offer insight on why it is so critical that we take the time to explore who we are, from a mind, body, spirit perspective.

Romantic Relationships

Though I didn't fully understand this concept in the beginning, I have now come to understand that every relationship I have attracted into my life came to teach me a lesson ***about myself***. I had no control over the actions of others, and the test was always in how I responded and reacted to each situation. It allowed me to discover the specific experience required of me at that moment.

I'm convinced that as we evolve, we will have multiple relationships with people I call "Soul Mates," and the person we choose to spend our lives with is our "Life Partner." The experience of each relationship, no matter how volatile or enchanting, is not wasted. It is in those moments when we do the most growing and maturing when we learn to navigate each situation not based on pure emotion or ego but through the vibration of love. I have nothing but gratitude for all of the "Soul Mates" I have attracted on my journey thus far.

YOUR REFLECTIONS
CHAPTER 3

Note: I understand this may be new information for you to digest and you may have spent the last few decades ignoring or unaware of the mother wound so, consider hiring a qualified therapist to offer you some tools to support your healing in this area.

Write about your relationship with your mother.
Was it loving or less than loving?

_____

_____

_____

_____

_____

_____

_____

_____

_____

wendicherry.com   @AwakenAndHeal

If you felt the tension growing up and your mother is alive, do you feel comfortable talking to her about her physical, emotional, and mental state when you were in utero?

If yes, write down three questions you would ask her about that time in her life.

_____

_____

_____

_____

_____

If no, spend some time in prayer and meditation asking for guidance on how to navigate this situation. Consider sharing your thoughts with your partner, a family member, or friend.

_____

_____

_____

_____

_____

Write about your first love.
How did you meet?
How did the relationship make you feel?
What is the status of your relationship with this person now?

_____

_____

_____

_____

_____

Write about your first heartbreak.
How old were you and how long did it take for you to recover from it?
Honestly, have you recovered from it?

_____
_____
_____
_____
_____

Describe your feelings and emotions about that time in your life.

_____
_____
_____
_____
_____

What is your truth in your current love relationship?

_____
_____
_____
_____
_____

What lesson is your current partner in your life to teach you in this moment?

_____
_____
_____
_____
_____

Letter to My Soul Mates

Dear Soul Mate,

I forgive you.

Please forgive me for any way I may have caused you harm.

Though we may have hurt each other, I now understand that we were brought together, in that specific season, to learn lessons about ourselves. We were only using the tools and information we had at the moment that we experienced our relationship. We both made mistakes during our time together and I finally and wholeheartedly release you in love.

You are an awesome wonder, created by God. I pray that you have abundant peace, pleasure, and prosperity on the next leg of your journey.

In gratitude.

Your name

wendicherry.com   @AwakenAndHeal

Chapter 4: Woe Is My Womb

"I think I made a wrong turn back there somewhere" – Erykah

Badu

My first menstrual cycle had begun one particular morning when I was in the sixth grade – I was 12. Though I wasn't in anticipation or particularly excited for her arrival, Mommy had given us books to educate us, so I *technically* knew what to expect. Even more than that, I knew not to bring any babies into the house as a teenager.

By that afternoon, after school, I was balled-up on the bathroom floor, not understanding what this new and horrible pain in my belly was. My mom, teachers, and a few experienced friends had given me the 'period talk,' but no one had ever mentioned anything about pain. The nausea was so intense; it held me hostage on the floor of the bathroom. The pain was severe for the entire five days of each cycle; I hadn't signed up for this. I missed many days of school and even got sick on the morning of my SAT. I was unable to get out of bed to take the test because of those damn cramps. I liken the pain to a freight train, moving top-speed right through my uterus so intensely, it would force me to vomit. Nausea became my middle name, and I loathed the salty taste that would form in my mouth right before I lost my lunch.

That unbearable pain became a 'normal' part of my life, throughout middle school, high school, and college, forcing me to plan my entire life based on when my cycle would come. I had to put everything on hold until after my period; otherwise, I had no control of the potential blood bath. I'd ruined so many pairs of underwear, pants, skirts, towels, and bedsheets over the years. In high school, my gynecologist prescribed 800 milligrams of Motrin. Soon afterward, she worried because, after so many years, the lining in my stomach could potentially be compromised. So, she switched me to birth control pills in college, but those made me even sicker. I hated sleeping away from home when I was on my cycle for fear of unleashing a blood bath on someone else's belongings.

This era in my life was the beginning of my war with my womb. We hadn't gotten off on the right foot. Over the years, each cycle gave me unbearable agony, ruined clothing, sheets, and evoked a major hate-hate complex. I knew a few people would say how poorly they felt during their cycles, but there was no one in my circle of friends who suffered the way I did. From middle school until I was in the working world, I looked for new ways to numb the pain and impact of these cramps. Though everyone was sympathetic to my plight, they had no clue of the depths of the physical and emotional anguish my monthly cycle unleashed on me. Ultimately, the 800 milligrams of Motrin became my drug of choice, and life went on.

The diagnosis of fibroids in April of 1996, was the first time I heard of the term. I was 20-something, traveling, and enjoying life. I was an event manager on the Commodore Cruise Line, a Western Caribbean cruise line whose main port was The River Walk, in New Orleans, Louisiana (NOLA). Our 'run' included ports in Cozumel, Mexico on Mondays, the Grand Cayman Islands on Tuesdays, Montego Bay, Jamaica on Wednesdays, and back to NOLA to repeat the 7-day circuit all over again, each Saturday.

It was exciting at first. Every Monday, I'd disembark the ship in Cozumel, Mexico to sit at the bar at Carlos and Charlie's restaurant. I watched MTV to catch up on the newest music and pop culture in the states. The Fugees had just released their debut album, *The Score,* and one of my co-workers let me burn a copy. I was proud of my fellow New Jerseyans and kept them on rotation the whole trip. They gave me a little piece of home as I was home sick and in culture shock out on the high seas.

I'd only been aboard for two-months when one day while managing some events for the ship's "Junior Cruisers," I felt a pain in my side that took my breath away. The kiddies and I were inside of our cozy event space called, The Rainbow Room, which housed all of our games, entertainment center, and crafting supplies. There was also a 10-foot, retractable, royal red velvet, curtain to drape over the huge picture window, for when the waters got rough. On some days, the view from that picture window would reveal the most spectacular views of the sun or moon glistening on the water, other times, the water was so rough and choppy that many of us would get seasick by merely peering out of it.

So, when that sharp pain hit, I grabbed my side and slid down the edge of the velvet curtain to try to keep my balance but also trying not to rip the curtain down. Luckily, I just happened to be standing in front of the picture window when that pain tore through my side. I didn't want to alarm the children. So, I sat on the floor and draped the curtain over me while I inched my way over to the wall, to grab the ship's telephone, to call for help. The telephone automatically dialed the ship's operator, and I yelled, "Help!" when she picked up. By this point, it was becoming hard to breathe, and the pain was not subsiding. I'd never felt anything like this before.

The majority of the children were watching a movie except for one little 8-year old girl who'd had her eye on me the entire time. She walked over to check on me. "Miss Wendi, are you ok?" she asked in her thick Latin accent. I mustered a fake smile and nodded, yes. She offered me a fake smile back, knowing that I wasn't telling her the truth. Just in time, the ship's nurse, Tim, rushed in to check on me. Boy, was I glad to see him! He was the coolest nurse I knew. Tim was a tall, fit, English guy with a goat-tee, who always sported stylish shades. He was one of the co-workers I had on the ship that I shared meals and excursions with on our downtime.

He quickly gave me the once-over and suggested I head down to the basement to the ship's hospital so he could get a better assessment. It was only Saturday, which meant we were on day one of our seven-day cruise, and Sunday would be yet another day at sea before arriving in Cozumel on Monday morning.

After a few diagnostic tests, it was determined that I needed to have a pelvic ultrasound to get to the root of what was causing my pain. Of course, the ship's hospital did not have an ultrasound machine so, they suggested I stick it out over the next two days to make it to a clinic on Grand Cayman Island for the test. Tim knew that their clinic would have a sonogram machine, and I would receive a more superior level of care in that country.

As soon as we docked in Grand Cayman on that Tuesday, accompanied by Tim, I was whisked by tender and taxi to the clinic. "Was this tiny office the clinic?", I questioned. It looked like my high school nurse's office, where I'd spent many of my days, lying down on the cot due to cramps. The Caymanian doctor and nurse were very attentive and kind as they proceeded to administer my very uncomfortable pelvic ultrasound. On the screen, the doctor pointed to a few discolored areas on my ovaries, which indicated cysts. His diagnosis was that a cyst had ruptured, causing the pain. Then he told me that I'd had a few small fibroids as well. Fibroids and cysts? "What was this about?" I asked. That was a new term for me but one that I'd repeatedly hear over the next few decades. The doctor was uncertain how I'd 'gotten' these cysts and fibroids but told me to seek further care when I returned home to the US.

Hunter, Skye, and Bailey

The next year, I moved to the Washington, D.C., metropolitan area. My partner at the time and I had been glued to the TV, enjoying one of our favorite pastimes, a big pile of Maryland blue crabs. However, I was feeling a little nauseous, and as the day went on, I was declining rapidly. Simultaneously, splashed all across the TV was the news that John F. Kennedy, Jr. and his new wife had just perished in a plane accident. I, like many Americans, was shocked and saddened to see what had happened. We watched every report from every news station, wondering how such a tragedy could happen to what seemed like such a nice guy. His family had certainly seen its fair share of traumatic and unexpected deaths. I felt sad for him because nobody wanted to go out in such a disastrous way.

As sad as I was for him, profound nausea was beginning to creep into my belly, slowly making its way into my throat. This unbearable sensation quickly grasped my attention. I became extremely sensitive to the smells around me – even the delightful one of the Old Bay Seasoning was making me want to hurl. After a few hours, I was unable to move or hold down any food or even water; I'd attributed it to food poisoning from the crabs. I'd never felt so bad in my life. The hours stretched into days, and I was still unable to get out of bed. My partner took me to the doctor, where we found out that I was pregnant. I was mortified! Our relationship was not strong enough to withstand the pressures of an unplanned baby.

They sent me home, but the symptoms never subsided. As the days passed, I was never able to stay out of bed for long; I felt weak, nauseous, and started to look and feel emaciated. The doctors kept telling me to drink plenty of water and Ginger Ale and to eat soups and crackers. That was a joke! What didn't they get? Nothing, not even water would stay down before my body would violently throw it up. I had never felt nausea to this degree before. Again, I was fighting a losing battle, trying to get someone, anyone to understand what I was feeling. From the minute I opened my eyes each morning until the time I went to sleep, I felt like I was going downhill on a roller coaster ride. Finally, after one of the many doctor visits, a female doctor shared that she thought I might be suffering from *Hyperemesis Gravidarum (HG)*. "Hyper what?" "Gravi, who?" I weakly questioned. By that time, I was in survival mode and totally over it.

According to the Hyperemesis Education and Research Foundation (which did not exist when I was pregnant), Hyperemesis Gravidarum (HG) is a severe form of nausea and vomiting in pregnancy. Generally described as unrelenting, excessive pregnancy-related nausea, and or vomiting that prevents adequate intake of food and fluids.[8] If severe and or inadequately treated, it is typically associated with:

- loss of greater than 5 percent of pre-pregnancy body weight (usually over 10 percent)

- dehydration and production of ketones (A chemical substances that the body makes when it does not have enough insulin in the blood. When ketones build up in the body for a long time, severe illness or coma can result.)

- nutritional deficiencies and malnutrition

- difficulty with daily activities

I was a textbook case throwing up so much that I required multiple hospital visits to receive nutrition through an intravenous line (IV). I was frightened to hear that these symptoms could potentially last through the entire first trimester. Just the thought of that long-term prognosis and how miserably I was feeling led me to decide to have an abortion - much to the chagrin of my partner. This abortion wasn't an easy decision, but I was unapologetically in self-preservation mode. My partner and I argued a lot, there were a lot of tears, and I could feel the resentment emanating from him. However, I was determined to feel better by any means necessary. After all, I'd missed lots of work and had been holed up in the house bedridden for too long.

We arrived at the local abortion clinic and sat in a gray, cold, stark room with women of all ages and ethnicities. As I looked around, the one commonality I noticed was that we all looked petrified. I know I was…I'd had no idea what to expect and honestly had turned my nose up at women who admitted to having an abortion in the past. My mind was spinning, and I was confident that Jesus was going to crack the ceiling at any minute and strike me dead on the spot. I just wanted this experience over as soon as possible. Finally, they called my name, and to get this over with, I signed the necessary papers. I was feeling extremely nauseous, achy, and weak and in enough physical and emotional pain that I was willing to forge ahead even though I was sure that I was going straight to hell. "Wendi Cherry," the lady whispered out into the waiting room. I got up and followed her down a long hallway into a back room filled with another group of ladies. Some were sitting in chairs, others lying on tables – everyone looked numb.

Once in the back, I undressed and put on a dingy, white robe that closed in the back. I was shivering so much that the nurse gave me a brown blanket, just as dingy as the robe, and gray non-slip socks to put on my feet. I laid on the table and allowed the anesthesia to kick-in and lull me away from this nightmare. I woke up a bit sore but so thankful it was over. I rested for a while and could not wait to get the hell out of there. I still didn't feel 100 percent but was emotionally drained and ready to get home and into my bed. By the end of the night, I was back on this crazy roller coaster of nausea - I was feeling terrible. It felt like deja vu because I still couldn't hold down water or food. That familiar ache and sickness in the pit of my stomach crept back up into my throat. "What in the hell is happening?" I bawled to my partner. He looked just as puzzled as I was and immediately called the emergency nurse on duty to share my experience. She said to try to get some sleep and to come back in the morning, should the symptoms persist. After a hellish night, we rushed back to the clinic, a sonogram determined that they hadn't gotten everything the first time! "What do you mean you didn't get everything?" I shouted.

I was furious! I could not even wrap my brain around the fact that I had to go through that entire procedure again! "What is wrong with these people?" I asked my partner, not expecting an answer. Numb, nauseous and completely zoned-out, I found myself back on that got-damn table with new strangers looking over me, asking me to count backward from 10. "10...9...8...7...", I whispered and drifted back to sleep. Upon waking, the doctors told me that I'd been pregnant with twins. They got the first fetus during the first procedure, and since they hadn't done a sonogram afterward missed the fact that there was still another fetus in my womb.

The only consolation I had was that I could instantly feel the difference. I felt like my "normal" self again and was so grateful. I was so guilty for terminating the children in my womb but relieved that I was no longer sick and vowed that would never, ever happen to me again. I learned that the symptoms of Hyperemesis Gravidarum usually re-appear with each future pregnancy. I didn't need to hear anymore because I was utterly traumatized by that experience.

I'm embarrassed to admit that less than one year later, it did happen again. Ugh! One random day, I began to feel that familiar ache and sickness in the pit of my stomach, trying to creep up into my throat. I had been back on birth control for a while, even though it made me sick, so I am not sure how it happened. Nonetheless, I instantly knew what it was and without telling my partner decided to terminate this pregnancy too. He and I were already struggling in our relationship, and I knew he would try to talk me out of it. Shit...he wasn't the one throwing up and on this physical, emotional, and mental roller coaster so, I made an executive decision for *my* body. I toiled over the decision for a few more days, but in the end, I had a friend take me to get the abortion. A different clinic, same horror, same pained, glazed look on the other women's faces. "How the hell did I get myself in this situation...again?", I berated myself in my head. "10...9...8...7...", I whispered and drifted to sleep for round three. Upon waking, the doctors told me that I was 100 percent clear. Upon my arrival, I made it crystal clear that I expected that they only perform one procedure and that they take every precaution to ensure that I was not going to have to go through this upsetting experience again.

I didn't know it then, but I was causing so much trauma to my womb and my soul. I had no connection to my body, let alone the sacredness of my womb at that point. I just wanted the pain to end and hadn't considered any long-term emotional or physical issues these abortions would cause. I buried that experience deep in the recesses of my soul and kept it moving. I continued to suffer severely with my cycle over the years and figured it was just going to be my life until menopause.

The last straw was during an event that I was working on at The Lincoln Theater on U Street in Washington, D.C., that featured recording artist Patti LaBelle. Just as we were arriving on-site for our staff meeting, my period came unexpectedly. Slated to be a day-long event, I couldn't believe it…we'd just begun the soundcheck, and my period came suddenly. I'd even chosen to wear white pants that day.

I wasn't prepared and didn't have the time to buy anything, and none of the other ladies had a pad to spare. So, I reasoned that I'd be safe if I just stuffed my undies with toilet paper. So, I did, crossed my fingers and prayed for the best – after all, the show must go on. Ms. Patti was chatty and specific about what she wanted, and I was designated to take extra-special care of her.

As I was walking her to her dressing room, I felt a familiar "guuush" – oh, shit! I got her to her dressing room and hauled-ass to the bathroom just in time to see the blood gushing all over the floor and toilet. I knew I needed to get back to Ms. Patti so frantically worked to clean myself and the surrounding areas as swiftly as I could. I didn't want to leave a trace of my existence in that bathroom. I became a fixture in there over the next eight-hours, ensuring that I was as clean and contained as I could be. At that moment, I knew there was no way I could continue living like this. I just needed to figure out a plan.

That next week, I went directly to my gynecologist, who told me that I had seven fibroids taking up space in my uterus. I had no idea what that meant except that I should consider a new laser procedure to remove them. It was an outpatient surgery, which seemed easy enough, and the recovery time was minimal, so I went for it; however, during my 12-month post-check-up, I was told that the fibroids had come back - with a vengeance. I was disappointed because that surgery had been touted as the magic bullet, to resolve the problem.

So, after a few more years of blood baths, ruining more sheets, clothing, and soaking 5-6 sanitary napkins per day, I was desperate to learn of more options. My gynecologist performed two additional surgeries; however, in the end, the fibroids always returned larger and greater in number. I was at my wit's end, and as far as the gynecologist was concerned, my only other alternative was a hysterectomy. I knew I didn't want to be so aggressive, but my desperation placed it squarely at the top of the list of options.

There was a fibroid study held at the George Washington Hospital in Washington, D.C., around the same. Within weeks, I was sitting in a sterile hospital treatment room, answering a 4-page questionnaire. Moving forward, I would be considered patient #2. I reasoned that along with helping myself, I could be helping a large number of other women suffering from fibroids by participating in this ground-breaking study. So, I got undressed and put my feet in the stirrups and prayed for the best.

"Wendi...Wendi!" from a distance, I heard someone calling my name. I felt dizzy and had no idea what was happening. When I came back to myself, I realized that I was lying on the cold, hard floor. I had passed out as soon as the surgical team attempted to insert the scapula. I do remember experiencing a lot of pain during the beginning part of the procedure, but apparently, the pain was so intense that I had passed out. The doctors and nurses were scrambling around, trying to figure out what was wrong with me.

I'd made the medical team aware of my vasovagal syncope once they got me back on the table. I kept throwing up and as compassionate as they tried to be, they kept rushing me to get dressed so they could bring in the next patient. I felt terrible and could not pull myself together. I was having a hard time standing up, let alone getting dressed, and there was no way I was going to make it to my car, which was blocks away. They helped me up, got me some water, and put me in an empty room where I could lay down until a friend could come to get me. They also told me that they'd concluded that because I had so much scar tissue, I was not the right candidate for their study. "What am I supposed to do now?" I queried. "Go back to your gynecologist.", the doctor said before scurrying out, leaving me nauseous and with more questions than ever.

I went on with life, trying to make that time of the month as comfortable for myself as possible, but those freight-train like pains offered no mercy. I'd already spent so much financial and emotional currency and time focusing on this issue. It was becoming clear that the doctors weren't sure about the creation of fibroids, let alone how to get rid of them.

I was still desperate for relief, by any means necessary so, I decided to move ahead with the hysterectomy. The day before I was planning to make my appointment, I saw a story on the news where specific surgical instruments used for that procedure, were proving to cause cancer in women. That stopped me dead in my tracks, and I decided my search would have to continue.

Sound Scape: "Didn't Cha Know" by Erykah Badu

Searching
(Photo: Derrick Watkins, 2012)

My Discoveries & Reflections

Not only did I not grieve my abortions, honestly, I felt more relief than sadness. After those procedures, I'd suppressed the emotions down into the deepest parts of my soul, hoping to forget that experience forever. In those days, I was not interested in being a mother. I never felt that mothering instinct kick in like it had for so many of my friends. While everyone around me was getting married and having babies, I was plotting my next international trip or career move. I'd seen the 'baby father drama' play out with a few of my acquaintances and through the media – so, I felt like I'd escaped the madness. Though I always anticipated the coming of my monthly cycle with much dread, it had only exacerbated as I aged. One doctor even told me things would improve after my first child, but that wasn't the case for me.

I felt trapped after the doctors at George Washington Hospital were unable to help me. "How in the world was I supposed to wait, at the minimum, twelve-more years for menopause to kick in?" I wondered. It wasn't until many years later that I would begin to consider that some of my womb issues could have been passed down to me. I began to learn about transgenerational trauma mostly studied amongst Native Americans and Holocaust survivors.[9] Though there are fewer studies, be clear, melanated peoples have survived an African Holocaust. Many of us are still carrying the pain and anguish of our ancestors, as taught by Native Americans, who believe that transgenerational trauma can be passed down at least seven generations. According to the author, Molly Larkin, the "7th generation" principle says that in *every decision*, be it personal, governmental, or corporate, we must *consider how it will affect our descendants* seven generations into the future. [10]

I had what I consider a double-whammy. In addition to the fibroids, I learned that there was such a thing called 'grief after abortion.' I was learning that the mind and the heart forgive for us to keep functioning, but the body keeps the record – the body not only tells a story, it also tells history. Even though outwardly, I hadn't given a second thought to my abortions, my body grieved them, causing stagnancy, which in turn may have been one of the contributing factors of my fibroids.

In Dr. Christiane Northrup's book, *Women's Bodies, Women's Wisdom* (2010), she notes that "not having fully grieved a pregnancy termination can be a setup for pregnancy problems in the future because of the unresolved feelings surrounding the choice." Professional Therapist Trudy M. Johnson, L.M.F.T., who helps women with grief after an abortion decision, believes women do not typically talk about an abortion in their past, "This is because they don't want to risk rejection, receive condemnation, or be misunderstood about the natural sadness that can occur after a voluntary pregnancy termination." Women experience something called disenfranchised grief, which is grief experienced by an individual that is not openly acknowledged, socially validated, or publicly observed.[11] Traditionally after an abortion, there are no open venues to talk about it, cry about, or express any emotion over the feeling of loss.

According to a 2015 abortion study by the Centers for Disease Control (CDC):[12]

- Among the 49 reporting areas that provided data for 2015, a total of 638,169 abortions were reported.

- Women in their 20s accounted for the majority (58.7 percent) of abortions and had the highest abortion rates.

- In 2015, 14.3 percent of all women who obtained an abortion were married, and 85.7 percent were unmarried.

These statistics prove that there needs to be a larger, all-encompassing conversation on this topic between the sexes. In my opinion, the stigma needs to be removed, and the shame lifted so those men and women needing healing and support feel comfortable seeking it out.

YOUR REFLECTIONS
CHAPTER 4

Have you experienced trauma to your womb? (i.e., abortions, rape, poor sexual choices)

What healing modalities have you either tried or are you considering?

_____

_____

_____

_____

_____

Do you have fibroids, PCOS, or other womb issues?

_____

_____

_____

_____

_____

wendicherry.com   @AwakenAndHeal

Describe your relationship with your womb.

_____
_____
_____
_____
_____

If you believe that you are experiencing womb issues, what is the one next step you can take by month's end to get support?

_____
_____
_____
_____
_____

Our wombs are our creative center. We are either birthing a baby, an idea, or a business.

Write down three creative ideas you have been considering.

What are the two next steps you can do to move them along by week's end?

_____
_____
_____
_____
_____

Chapter 5: Dead Woman Walking

"We can pray to early May, fast for 30 days, still it won't let go."
– Erykah Badu

"Yooo, y'aaalll, I'm about to hit I-95 South; so, keep your mouths shut!" It was right there, at the tip of my tongue…I kind'a whispered it out loud a few times but not loud enough for anyone to hear me. I must have been feeling what every other potential run-away bride or groom feels, just minutes before they decide to head for the hills. I was too terrified to pull the trigger. My family was in town from California. Someone had already bought the china set from my Bed, Bath and Beyond registry. A whole posse of my future in-laws made their way from down south and up north to celebrate the occasion.

It was my bachelorette party, and my two sisters, Aimee and Erinn plus Cheryl (Chers) and Wanda, were staying the night with me in the bridal suite. We'd had a long night of the customary rehearsal and dinner, then the entire bridal party headed out to the popular nightclub, Republic Gardens on U Street in D.C., to party some more. So, though I enjoyed partying with everyone, my extreme guilt would not allow me to utter those words and haul-ass doing 100 MPH down I-95 South.

This was just a few weeks after the horrible September 11th terror attacks took the U.S. by surprise, and the week before that, on the morning of my bridal shower, the singer Aaliyah died. Needless to say, while the nation was grieving, I was having survivor's remorse and didn't have the courage or dare make such an emotional decision as to roll-out the night before my wedding. Truth be told, I'd known for the last year that I didn't want to get married but felt pressure as I was over 30-years-old and he was, as everyone loved pointing out, a great guy. I certainly didn't dispute that – he was a great guy. Funny, handsome, charismatic, giving, loving, sensitive; still, I could not get that feeling of disconnection out of the pit of my stomach. So, I tried harder…I prayed, cried, fasted, went to church, and did everything I knew in my power to do to *force* myself to fall in love. I now know as I knew then, that is impossible, but I kept at it. In some circles, they say someone should love you more than you love them – what a load of crap! In the end, those words stayed lodged in my throat the entire night, and after a while, I chose to choke them down whole. I felt at this point, there was no way out but to go through with this wedding.

I was a bundle of nerves the next day but pulled it together to get dressed and greet the well-wishers, coming in and out of my bridal suite. All of my loved ones, including Auntie, were there, and I was grateful for that. She'd been one of the ones continuously asking, "When is this wedding going to happen?" It was time to go downstairs to the ballroom for the ceremony. So, there I was in my belly-revealing, white, sheer wedding dress, standing next to my Dad in the doorway. I noticed that he seemed disoriented as I saw his bloodshot eyes darting around. He wasn't his usual loud, jokester self that I was relying on to get me down the aisle. His wife leaned in and whispered to me that he was in the beginning stages of Parkinson's Disease. Ugh! No wonder he seemed a bit off. I knew I'd never seen him behave in this manner before, but at this moment, standing in the door, waiting to make my entrance or throw up, there was no time to analyze the situation. I felt obligated to walk up this aisle, with a smile on my face, so walk I did. I was in a haze, walking to meet my future husband and the wedding party, who were all smiling so radiantly at me.

Out of the corner of my left eye, I saw my Delta Line Sister, Sharriff, beaming at me. Next, I noticed my God-Sister, Jordan, sporting a cool afro and goggle-styled red shades. I was intrigued by her new look. Therefore, for me not to turn around and run like a bat-out-of-hell, I kept my focus on her as I walked up the aisle. My Dad was no support because he was having trouble walking, so I had to drag him along. It felt like forever, but I'd finally made it to the platform stage to greet the pastor, my bridal party, and intended.

"What the f*ck am I doing?!", I questioned myself. My belly and my feet were tingling at the same time. I shifted from side to side because my feet were hurting so badly. I was starting to get that familiar salty taste in my mouth. I prayed in my head, "Lord, no! Please, don't let me pass out on this stage!" I didn't know what to do or where to focus. Thankfully, at that moment, my one-year-old niece, Ariana, let out a piercing scream grabbing everyone's attention – though short, it was a welcomed distraction. The poor baby was teething and had an ear infection so, Mommy escorted her out. Like baby Ariana, I wanted to scream too, "Mommy, don't leave me!" But, she was out of range by then so, I forged onward.

The ceremony probably lasted about 15-minutes or so, but I was utterly tuned-out into another universe. Being paralyzed by the sheer fear of the gravity of the situation, honestly, I don't know how I kept it all together. The rest of the ceremony and reception went on as planned. We went around and did what I called the grip-and-grin, greeting all of our guests. We were very meticulous about our guest list, so each encounter brought about encouraging energy. We also did the customary, daddy-daughter and couple's first dances, the "Delta Sweetheart Song," the "Electric Slide," the cake cutting, and throwing of the bouquet though I felt like a zombie just going thru the motions; frozen in this experience and afraid of what the future held. What had I just done?

In those days, I was emotionally disconnected from my body. I didn't know about intuition, the fact that my body was sending me signals to tell me whether or not I was going in the right direction. At that point, I probably would not have listened and even worse trusted those signals. The norm was to doing things other people wanted me to. What I knew for sure was that I was *not* in love. I did not have that authentic soul connection deep inside my gut, and I felt like there was nothing I could *do* about it. I knew it pretty early on in the relationship, but because it had never happened before, I thought it was something that I could grow into as time passed. I could not wrap my head around why I was not feeling anything. The harder part was trying to get him and those around me to understand what I was feeling, which was difficult because I didn't have a concrete reason why. I kept trying to wish it away, change it, and made excuses for my lack of it. Over the next couple of years, I felt numb and joyless. The color of the sky, trees, and flowers faded. The taste of food, the sound of music, the enjoyment of friends and family all turned a dark shade of gray. At the end of the day, I was a dead woman walking.

Intuition

Like usual, I forged ahead with life, refusing to listen to my intuition, which continually signaled to me that I had made a wrong choice. I would come home every day from work, exhausted, overwhelmed, and sad. As soon as I got home each day, I'd roll into the fetal position in my bed. From the time I got in the car to begin my long commute until I made that left into my complex, I could barely breathe. I was dreading going home but figured I'd made my bed, so I had to lay in it. I prayed that I would be able to build a spiritual, emotional connection with my husband – but it never happened. I loved his personality, what he stood for, his family, and other noble qualities, but I wasn't *in* love with him — big difference. In my opinion, there is a sense of peace, ease, a natural flow, a feeling of deep connection when two people are in an authentically loving relationship. The Teddy Pendergrass lyrics that stuck in my head the most were from a song called, "When Somebody Loves You Back" and rang so true for my situation.

"It's so good lovin' somebody…"

"When somebody loves you back and that's a fact."

"Said not 70-30…"

"Not 60-40…"

"Talkin' 'bout a 50-50 love…"

Nevertheless, I was somebody's wife! What in the hell was I doing? I wasn't even a great cook or housekeeper. I was used to life on the road, having traveled for the majority of my time right after college and before settling in Washington, D.C. in 1997. I was a roadie, I'd lived in hotels and on the ship, I'd had chefs and room stewards, so I was a bit out of touch with the reality of what being a wife meant. We struggled from day one, and he became resentful as we both realized that nothing was changing. Unfortunately, we stayed on the hamster wheel, just going along to get along.

#TheSydSyd

Then, one day, I'd begun to feel that familiar, sick, nausea in the pit of my stomach. "You've got to be kidding me!" I thought to myself. We were down south in my husband's hometown for a funeral. It was a sad occasion, so I tried to offer as much support as I could. Everyone else had gotten up for church, but I literally could not move. As soon as I'd opened my eyes, I felt like I was traveling 90 MPH down the hill of a roller coaster. To make matters worse that southern heat and soupy humidity had already started to kick-in, making things worse. No matter what I tried, I could not get out of bed.

I so hated to miss church services with the family. Once everyone got home from church, my sisters-in-law started asking me questions, coyly suggesting that I might be pregnant. "Oh, my God!" "Me, a mom?" I questioned. I'd only told my mom and sisters about my past pregnancy experiences. I mean, that wasn't something I was particularly proud of, nor was it anyone else's damn business. So, we all sat around the kitchen table, and they each shared their war stories about being pregnant and in labor. I was not amused or excited. It all scared the crap out of me. I had a few more rough days before getting home to my doctor, who had confirmed what I was suspecting. I was pregnant...again. This time, I promised myself that I would carry the pregnancy to term, by any means necessary.

I had to emotionally and physically prepare myself for the roller coaster rides and violent vomiting that began to consume my daily life. I was already at seven weeks, and the doctors mentioned that I might start feeling better by week 12, the beginning of the second trimester. Unfortunately, I had no such luck. I had to make several trips per week to the urgent care, for bags of fluid to support my chronic dehydration. At this point, the doctors made the decision that I would get a permanent intravenous (IV) pic port put into a vein in my arm – ugh. I was deathly afraid of needles! I'd been stuck so many times that all of my veins had "blown." Meaning, they were unable to draw blood from a 'good vein' to administer the IV. Each night, I had to attach the bag of fluids to my IV port 12 hours per day – from 7 p.m. to 7 a.m., refreshing the bag one time in the middle of the night. It was a terrible and painful experience. I kept a bandage on my pic line during the day to ensure the line didn't get pulled out or infected.

I'd even had to take a leave from work for a month because I was so violently ill. I was home alone while my husband was at work. I tried to eat, but nothing would stay down. I was losing weight rapidly but was determined to carry this baby to term. Not only couldn't I keep food or drink down, but I also had an aversion to certain smells, including mints and cologne. I felt like my body was playing tricks on me. Was God punishing me for my two prior abortions? Though most people were empathetic to my plight, there was not one single person who could feel my pain. It was hard to explain, and the doctors had no solutions and almost made me feel like this was all in my head. I felt angry, sad, isolated, unsure, and terrified of the next six months. I wasn't sure I would be able to endure this level of suffering for such an extended period.

Eventually, I had to get back to work. We'd just purchased a home and needed the additional income. So, I would drag myself out of bed, detach my IV at 7 a.m., shower, then get on the beltway to drive more than an hour each way, from Silver Spring, Maryland to Falls Church, Virginia, to my office. I constantly had to spit, so I carried a spit cup and can of chocolate flavored Boost (the only thing that would stay down) with me each morning. My co-workers, mostly women, were very understanding and knew to clear the way when they saw me running to the bathroom, to offer up yet another meal to the porcelain gods.

My sister-in-law called me one day and told me to pull myself together; she suggested I cut my meals in half. To consume one portion and throw it up, if needed and try to eat the other part later. That way, I would quell the rapid amount of weight I was losing. I was down to 120 pounds from my typical weight of 130 pounds and becoming emaciated; my usually full cheeks were beginning to sink in, and my eyes were starting to bulge. Oddly enough, my hair was growing like weeds and became even longer and thicker.

One day, while sitting at my desk, I felt a tiny flutter in the pit of my belly. "Wow!" I said out loud to myself. It happened again, and I told my intern what was happening. It was the first time I'd felt an actual connection to this little *"thing"* growing inside of me. Before that, I'd only felt resentment and anger towards *"it"* for making me so sick. I also was afraid that I wouldn't be able to travel and get-up-and-go at will. For I was a butterfly, a nomad, and didn't like the feeling of being held back or tied down. I needed to be free to flutter when and where I wanted. In my opinion, a baby was going to slow my roll *waaay* down, and I wasn't interested in that. However, with that one little kick, I felt an instant softening of my emotions and began to feel a sense of connection with the 'little bean' growing inside of me. I started to read the dozens of books Mommy had given me about pregnancy and parenthood. I could now gauge the size of the baby from the photos in the book. I was eager to find out the sex.

I had my fingers crossed for a girl. My husband already had children from a previous relationship, so he just wanted a healthy baby.

Finally, the day came for my sonogram to determine the sex. I was ecstatic when the ultrasound technician told me it was a girl! She gave me the black and white ultrasound photo with the words "Hi Mom" typed in the corner. The baby was sucking her thumb in utero and had the biggest head. I instantly started worrying about how I was going to push that big head out of me. We decided to call her Sydni, which is a derivative of the spelling of my name, adding the letter "i" at the end. Mommy gave her the middle name Jaiden, which during that time was the most popular in the United States.

From then on, I just called her by her name – Sydni Jaiden. The doctors warned that sometimes sonograms weren't accurate, but I knew in my gut, I was having a baby girl. I was thinking of all of the cute outfits she could wear, the things I would teach her, and the things we could do together. I was excited about the possibilities, even though the effects of my HG were as relentless as ever. I went through many ups-and-downs during that pregnancy. I felt isolated and alone, unable to go out, other than to go to work only to come straight home to get back in the bed. My body was changing in so many uncomfortable ways. This was not the glamorous pregnancy I saw the ladies experience on TV. A bonus, however, was that my older sister, Erinn, was pregnant at the same time. So, though she wasn't as sick as me or in the same type of relationship as me, we still bonded over the hopes, dreams, and possibilities of our unborn babies growing up as sister-cousins. Every day, we talked on the phone about what was happening with our pregnancies, work, and relationships.

My husband decorated the nursery beautifully, in my favorite color of lavender, with a Noah's Ark theme. We had her name spelled out across the wall, the cutest crib, linens, and chest-of-drawers. I washed all of her new clothes, onesies, and baby socks and tucked them neatly away. We excitedly assembled the glider rocker, and I would sit in her room, rocking back and forth, awaiting her arrival. I never fully recovered from the sickness but had no other choice but to suck it up. I learned that HG causes the baby to act as a parasite on the mom, and since she was healthy, I just had to hang on a little longer until she decided to make her appearance. The months crept along slowly, and at some point, I began having

Braxton-Hicks contractions four weeks before her due date. Wait…it wasn't time! Sydni's lungs weren't fully developed yet, so back to the obstetrician I went. She wanted Sydni to stay put, at least another three weeks, for her lungs to develop more. So, she placed a few stitches in my uterus to ensure Sydni didn't slide out before her time. So, for the next few weeks, I walked around like a penguin, so sure that at any moment, I would see her hand pop out between my legs. Her head was facing down, directly into the birth cannel, and I felt every bit of it. Two weeks later, the stitches had dissolved on their own, and the doctor told me it was safe for her to come at any time.

Even though I was still sick every day, I was not ready for Sydni to arrive in this crazy world. There was a sniper on the loose in the Washington, D.C. metropolitan area. Several people were randomly killed, and unfortunately, many of the shootings happened in the areas I frequented. A murder of an older gentleman took place at a gas station near my Silver Spring home. Another murder of a woman took place at the Home Depot in Falls Church, Virginia, which was near my job. I felt like I couldn't escape these crazies. There was no rhyme-or-reason to the shootings. The sniper killed black, white, young, old, women, men, and even shot a 13-year-old boy named Iran Brown. I felt like a moving target with such a big belly. Citizens walked in a zig-zag fashion every time they moved from their cars to a building, making it harder for the snipers to get a good shot. I felt crazy every time I moved from place to place, but everyone was in self-preservation mode, the fear hanging over the city was palpable.

I prayed hard that if I could zig-zag fast enough and keep her inside my belly, she would be safe. On October 24th, only two days before my birthday, and three weeks before Sydni was born, thankfully, the police caught the snipers, John Allen Mohammed and Lee Boyd Malvo. I considered that one of the best birthday gifts ever. The entire Metro-area was able to relax and breath after the traumatic experience of fearing for our lives daily. Heightening my fear, only six days later, on October 30th, DJ Jam Master Jay, the DJ from the hip-hop group, Run DMC, was murdered and police claimed that they didn't have any suspects. These stories infiltrated the news headlines every night. I wondered if the world was cracking up? With what was happening in the world and my home, my anxiety was becoming crushing.

We were in get-it-done mode, this particular Thursday around the office. Our team of event producers was working feverishly to get this last batch of mailings out before the post office closed. I felt full and tight so, I was sitting at my desk doing my part. We were a good team and made the deadline...so, I clocked out early and went home. That night, I drank my dinner...that damn can of chocolate Boost and went to sleep in the guest bedroom. I'd been having major leg cramps, night sweats, heartburn, and was plain miserable as my belly started to stretch and grow beyond what I thought I could tolerate. Once asleep, I began dreaming that my sister Aimee and I were at the doctor's office, and I was going to get a final sonogram. The doctor yelled, "It's a girl!" and in that very moment, I felt a pop inside of my head...or was it in my lower extremities? I couldn't tell if I was still dreaming. I woke up and realized this was not a dream. That "pop" I thought was in my head was my water breaking. The bed was soaked, the fluid was warm, and I felt like I'd just peed the bed.

During my pregnancy, I'd become a rabid fan of "A Baby Story" on Lifetime TV and knew that I needed to get a shower curtain and some towels under me, pronto. Having been warned that the amniotic fluid would stain the carpets, I made my way to the linen closet, draped myself with a towel, and limped into the master bedroom to tell my husband it was time to go to emergency. Sydni was on her way!

Luckily my hospital bag was already packed and at the door - thanks to "A Baby Story." I hadn't even had a chance to try to brush my teeth or jump in the shower before the first contraction came and dropped me to the floor, halfway between the closet and bedroom door. Oh, my God! I hadn't felt pain like that before. It was like having my worst menstrual cramps but on steroids. I'd seen the expectant moms crying and carrying on, and now I knew why - that pain was serious business. In between contractions, I called Mommy and Erinn to tell them to start making their way down I-95 south from New Jersey because Sydni was coming! Once at the hospital, the contractions came even quicker. I had no shame in my game. I wanted that epidural and with the quickness. Also, though I tried to warn the nurse that I had rolling veins, that blew and that she needed to be very careful when starting my IV, she didn't listen and missed the first attempt.

I was in pain and pissed off because I'd just told her ass to be careful, that I only wanted one stick! She was sweating so much that she had to bring in another nurse to hook up my IV. Soon after, the medicine was kicking in, and I was beginning to feel more relaxed. Over the last few months, my husband and I had not been getting along, so at that moment, he was merely a fixture in my room and offered no real emotional or spiritual support at all. When writing up my birthing plan, I'd requested my cousin, Wanda, and Chers, to join me in the delivery room. As fate would have it, neither of them were able to make it in time for the actual delivery so, there I was, in this delivery room, fighting back the tears, feeling alone, wondering, "How in the hell did I let myself get here?!"

That epidural was powerful so, I felt absolutely nothing as I lay there, watching TV. It was a beautiful but chilly November day, and watching "A Baby Story," taught me how to be aware of the machines and numbers on the monitors. Being informed of what to expect during my delivery, they weren't going to catch me slipping – or so I thought. Within the hour, it was time to start pushing. I knew to bare my chin into my chest and push down, but I was so numb I couldn't feel anything. The doctor's team kept yelling at me to "PUUUSH!" and I thought…I AM! There was a TV right in front of me, and somehow, amidst all of this commotion, my eye caught the CNN crawler along the bottom of the screen which read *"Killer of actor, Merlin Santana, charged with first-degree murder in Los Angeles."* How sad was that?! Merlin Santana had played a character on the "Steve Harvey Show" and had been senselessly murdered the week before. At that moment, I became aware of the fact that I was bringing a new life into the world, just as Merlin's family had to lay him to rest. I hadn't even seen my Sydni yet but already couldn't fathom losing her. Noticing I was distracted from pushing, the doctors turned off the TV and put a mirror right in front of me just in time for me to see the crowning of her head.

I pushed a few more times, and out she came – thank God, I physically felt better immediately. It was like a fairy godmother had waved her wand over my body and gold stars, green clovers, and blue diamonds appeared over my head like a rainbow. I can't explain it other than I felt back to normal. This little creature, with a gigantic knot on the side of her forehead, had finally popped out. I'd been in labor a total of five hours from the time my water broke until the time I was holding her in my arms. I guess God knew I'd already endured enough pain and had spared me long-drawn-out labor. Much to my chagrin, she looked just like her Dad. After all of this work, she didn't even look like me?! My feelings were hurt.

My dream was to have a baby girl that looked just like me. Due to being adopted, I didn't look like anyone else besides my biological sister. I was counting on Sydni to be my doppelganger. They immediately placed her on my belly, and I examined her in awe. Her little naked body was super slippery and pink. I also noted a large green blotch right on her butt. Ha! Despite not looking like me, she had the same birthmark as me, which felt pretty amazing. They whisked her away and began preparing me to push out the placenta. I was exhausted but relieved. She was here and healthy.

Chers had finally made it to the hospital. It seems that right at the moment I'd gone into labor, she'd been in a meeting and unable to make it. She brought a purple, plush hippopotamus along with her – Sydni's first stuffed animal. Chers was technically the first person, besides my husband and me who got to see Sydni after birth. Though seven months pregnant herself, my older sister, Erinn, finally made it to the hospital from New Jersey. I was relieved to have some support finally.

My husband headed back to the house to sleep as he was exhausted as well. I was so grateful for all of the calls of congratulations that flooded the hospital that day. They brought Sydni in for me to begin nursing, but that proved to be more painful than I could have ever imagined. The rest of that day was a blur, and I just knew that I was glad that Sydni was finally here. Since we were so close to Thanksgiving, my first meal after birth was turkey, mashed potatoes, green beans, and stuffing! When I say that bland hospital food tasted like steak and lobster, I was not kidding. I devoured that plate like I hadn't eaten in months because really, I hadn't.

With visiting hours over, it was the first time I'd gotten to spend time with Sydni alone. In my birthing plan, I noted that I'd wanted her to sleep in the room with me on the first night. Again "A Baby Story" served as an excellent education for me because it suggested that I learn her moans, coos, and cries while I could still get support from the nurses. There she was, lying swaddled next to me in her plastic bassinette with a blue and pink baby hat on her head. It was dark save for the TV light flickering in the background. I was lying there in a complete fog thinking, "What was I going to do with a baby?" I whispered her name, "Sydni Jaiden." She had to be familiar with it because I'd called her name so many times while she was in utero. No lie, right then, she turned her head in slow-motion, just like a robot and looked directly at me, with her dark eyes wide open. I couldn't believe what was happening and no one else was there to witness it. This baby had turned her head and was looking directly at me. Honestly, she was scaring the crap out of me, she stared, eyes wide open, for a little while then slowly turned her head back center. It was as if she was saying, "Mommy, chill out. Everything is going to be ok." I was stunned! What in the heck had just happened?

Once we got her home, it was all about trying to get her to nurse. She wasn't latching and I was in considerable pain. My nipples were sore, chafed, and cracking, and I got anxious every time I heard that smacking sound, indicating she was ready to eat. It seemed like every five minutes, she was smacking! Ugh! I felt shooting pains down my spine, every time I tried to get her to latch correctly, the way they'd taught me in my lactation class. Understanding the benefits of nursing, I'd wanted to nurse for as long as I could. I tried my best but was unable to tell how much she was drinking so I just kept at it.

My sister, Erinn and I were intrigued because we'd both waited so long to see what these babies were going to look like. At one point, she noted that besides me, Sydni was her first true blood relative who she knew. That was a powerful consideration, things only an adoptee would understand. She even nicknamed Sydni, "Smacks", due to the ever-present sound of smacking in the background. That baby was hungry, and I was doing my best to keep up.

I was so relieved when Mommy got to my home; I needed physical and emotional support at this point. I was overwhelmed, fatigued, and sore and to make matters worse, I had received a second-degree tear during delivery. I was having trouble sleeping and trying to stay on Smacks' nursing schedule. Overall, she was a pleasant baby, and I was trying to learn her personality. She only cried when she needed something and mostly just laid there like a bump on a log. A steady stream of visitors stopped by over the next few weeks to lavish her with gifts, snuggles, and love. This was supposed to be a celebratory time, but inside, I was filled with anxiety about what the future held. As usual, I moved forward and prayed for the best.

"No, Mama, please, Mama!" No, Mama, please, Mama!" In my head, I was screaming in my Penny from the 70s sitcom, "Good Times" voice – in my head that is. I wouldn't dare scream out loud. Mommy was heading back to New Jersey after coming for a few days to help me with Sydni. Hell, I ain't know nothing about birthing no babies and I did not want my mom to leave. It was taking everything in me not to execute that dive-move straight for her ankles that I had been visualizing over the last 24-hours. She would have been limping out of the door with that one free leg and dragging me down the driveway with the other. I was exhausted and frankly scared. What was I supposed to do with this little creature staring back at me from her rocker? I dared not make that plea out loud or else my mother would have felt so stressed that she may have tried to stay a little longer. Alas, I let her go and ran back upstairs to the kitchen window to watch her drive away through my tear-filled eyes. I glanced back over at my two-week-old baby girl, innocently and seemingly unbothered swinging back and forth in her swing and idiotically asked her, "What 'us' gonna do now?"

"Get that baby a bottle NOW!" Sydni's pediatrician yelled out of the door. This was her second-week check-up, and after a few diagnostics, the doctor reported that Sydni's body was in starvation mode. Because she hadn't been latching well, she had become malnourished and was beginning to lose muscle mass. A nurse gave Sydni a tiny, 4 oz. bottle of formula, and she started smacking for dear life. She downed that bottle in two-minutes flat, so they gave her another. Damn! No wonder she continuously smacked her lips; my poor baby had been starving because I wasn't able to nurse properly, I felt so guilty. Thank God, her other vitals were on par with that of a two-week-old infant.

There was absolutely no way, I was going to put my body and emotions through that type of torture again. So, I elected to have a tubal ligation performed, six weeks after Sydni was born, to the chagrin of my husband. I had the outpatient, laparoscopic procedure, which took less than an hour. Trying to nurse and cuddle an active baby was tough because she kept kicking me in my surgical scar. Eventually, it healed up, and I tried hard to settle into my life as a new mother.

After only four weeks, I was back at work. For the first few months, I did what I had to do and pumped in my office. When I felt the tingling sensation of the "let down," (when a nursing mother's milk actively releases from the cells that produce and store the milk.[13]), my compassionate office mate, Ahram, would step out and place my handwritten "Pumping" sign on the door. I resorted to simulating nursing when I was at home for the bonding experience and bottle-fed her the milk that I'd pumped at work. I kept some and sent some with her to the babysitter's house. Unfortunately, I was emotionally unable to sustain that schedule when I went back to work after my supervisor burst into my office, knowing she saw the damn sign on the door, to ask a stupid question. There I was, holding the two horn-like pump cups up to my breasts. My mouth dropped, and eyes bulged, and so did hers. I sat, and she stood there frozen while the "woosh-woosh-woosh" sound of the breast pump blared in the background. She apologized profusely, and I just started crying. This was all too much, and since I didn't have any hands-on, local support, I threw in the nursing towel. I'd wished Mommy, or my sister or other family members lived close enough to help me with the day-to-day logistics of working, mothering, and being a wife.

By that point, the wife's job was falling by the way-side. We were both over it, over 'us,' whatever 'us' was.

From the start, Sydni was a sweet, pretty, smart, and active baby. She would wake up singing, looking at her Noah's Ark mobile spinning above her head in the crib. She would coo and gurgle, enjoying the simple things like playing with her feet and making raspberries with her spit, she always had a juicy mouth. Video camera in hand, I loved sneaking up on her in the crib, wanting to capture her in her essence. She was very intuitive, and as soon as she sensed either of us in the room, she would start fake-crying. We would take turns scooping her up for a kiss and snuggle time. She was so light and smelled so good.

I made up a song for her, which much to her chagrin, I still occasionally belt out when the spirit hits me…" Sydniiii Jai-den Ba-rra, Sydni Jaiden Ba-ray-hey-hey-hey! Sydni…Jaiden Barra! Sydni Jaiden Ba-raaayyy!' I added a clap, clap, clap on the hey-hey-hey part, which became her favorite part as she got older. She had lots of energy and was very affectionate. I would also sing "Beautiful" by Snoop Dogg featuring Pharrell to her.

"Beautiful…I just want you to know…"

"You're my favorite girl…"

We had our tummy time on the floor. I read to her as we rocked in the glider, and kissed her cheeks while she fell asleep in my arms each night. Bath times were with Daddy, you could hear them giggling and splashing water everywhere. After bath time, the bathroom was a mess! He would wash her hair then slick it down with baby oil making her look like a wet chicken. She was so loveable.

The reality of my marriage was still grim, just like the lyrics to the Erykah Badu song "I Want You":

"We can pray to early May, fast for 30 days; still it won't let go."

There was nothing I could do to change what my gut and soul were feeling, which was numb and dead. I could not go on like this for much longer. Sometimes we argued, sometimes we didn't; however, there was always underlying negative energy around us; I was clear it wasn't healthy for either of us or the baby. Aside from work, I was so isolated and miserable that I knew that I needed to do something to free myself. I was too embarrassed to tell my close friends the details of how I was feeling. I mean, after all, we looked like the perfect couple. A new house, new baby, and all of the trappings that society claims is a symbol of you "moving on up." It was a farce, and I needed to find myself and my peace by any means necessary.

One sunny, cold day, right before Christmas, I was at my wits-end, still learning how to be a mother, wife, and working woman but was struggling greatly. Things were always so tense in my home; my anxiety crawled from my belly into my throat every night when I heard the garage door going up – the alarm system would say, "Front door, open." Shit, I just knew something was about to pop off, so I tried to stay pleasant and keep my distance.

We'd built our home in a new complex in the White Oak section of Silver Spring, Maryland, and were one of a handful of other black people on our block. Our across-the-street neighbor was a young single mother with two elementary-aged boys. They came over to meet us when they moved in and again when Syd first came home from the hospital. Occasionally, we would say hi when we were outside getting into our cars and the like. On this particular day, I was leaving the house to allow myself a breath of fresh air when my neighbor came across the street to greet me. As soon as I rolled down my window to greet her, I broke into uncontrollable sobs. The dam had broken, and there I was boohooing right there in the middle of the street. She invited me to come over to her house to get myself together. I pulled back into the driveway and walked into her home to continue my cry fest.

She shared that she was recently divorced and could feel the familiar energy of discord in my home, on the handful of times that she visited. She said that she'd prayed things would improve for us once the baby came but could tell from our comings and goings that was not the case. For the next few hours, she allowed me to spill my entire guts right there in her living room. It felt like a major release, a way for me to excise the emotions I'd suppressed in my body. I'd felt so many emotions but had learned to keep them bottled up because I just wanted everything and everyone to be ok. I am forever grateful to my neighbor Janet for listening to me that day, I think she may have saved my life because up to that point I was so emotional and anxious that I was having thoughts of suicide. In my heart, that was the day that I decided I needed to remove myself from this situation that wasn't serving the highest good of either of us. At that moment, I knew I needed to devise a plan to save my life.

A Change Is Coming

By the time Sydni was 18-months-old, I'd moved out and begun living in a poorly-kept, split-level townhouse in Kingstowne, Virginia. I didn't care; though, I was just grateful to be closer to my good girlfriends. On my first night in my new place, my mom, girlfriends, and I cracked open a bottle of wine, and they offered me a toast for a prosperous and peaceful new beginning! I was so excited and was finally authentically peaceful. The down-side was that I was a true single-mother now, bearing the responsibility of the day-to-day on my own. My commute to work was long, but I'd found the most perfect baby sitter, near my house, to take care of my Sydni. Things were coming together nicely.

As fate would have it, less than two weeks in the new spot, that ole', squirmy Syd-Syd, one of her numerous nicknames, accidentally poked me in the eye, in the middle of the night. It hurt so badly that I was seeing stars and shot out of bed to have a look in the mirror. Thank God, I could see, Sydni had not gouged my eye out even though it certainly felt like it. I was up, so I figured I'd pee before I jumped back in the bed. The next thing I heard was a scream. Then another and another. "Huh?" I thought to myself. At that moment, I opened my eyes and realized that I was on my back, looking up at the ceiling. Oh, shit…I'd passed out again. What in the hell was going on?! Still light-headed, I jumped to my feet to check on Sydni.

As I approached her, she recoiled away from me. "Hey, Syd-Syd, it's Mommy," I whispered to her. "What's wrong?" I gently questioned. Sydni was standing up in the bed, looking at me with pure terror in her eyes and refused to let me touch her. As I was talking to her, I began to notice "sand" in my mouth. Now my head was spinning, how did I get "sand" in my mouth, I wondered. I stumbled back into the bathroom to look in the mirror and was horrified by my reflection. Blood was covering the entire right side of my face and hair. Where in the heck was this blood coming from? Then I realized that wasn't sand, on the inside of my mouth. Instantly, I felt a gaping hole, right in the front of my mouth, where my tooth should have been.

Oh, shit! It turns out, I'd had a vasovagal syncope episode while attempting to use the bathroom. It seemed as I was passing out, I hit my mouth on the corner of the marble sink and knocked my left, front tooth out. I was mortified! I looked just like the prizefighter, Leon Spinks. Oh, no! I became light-headed and made my way back to the bed to lie down. I was dazed and confused about what had transpired in less than three minutes. Though it was 4 a.m., I called Chers, who was there in a flash. She took me to the emergency room where I got a tetanus shot, some pain meds, and the directions to see my dentist as soon as possible. "Shiiit…" I thought that was a no-brainer, I knew I was too cute to rock that Leon look so, called my dentist as soon as they opened the next day.

I felt like I was back living in the Twilight Zone. I wasn't passionate about the work I was doing, my commute was exhausting, and the pay was pitiful. My estranged husband and I had started exploring divorce, which caused an extra level of strain on the relationship. I felt like a hamster running like hell on a wheel…going nowhere fast. Deep in my heart, I wanted a change but didn't know I had the power to do something about it. During a random church service, the guest pastor shared the old adage…" doing the same thing over and over and expecting a different result is insanity." I realized, over the last few years, I'd been acting like an insane woman, still giving in to the requests and demands of others. Being always perceived as the "goodie-two-shoes" or "a good church girl," behind the scenes, I had a history of letting my emotions get the best of me. I could even be irrational and even violent when pressed to my limit. This was no way to live, I was enjoying this new-found peace, in this new home, but my soul desired more.

That Sunday at church, I decided quietly within myself, that I would immediately begin to do things differently. Instead of meeting my soon-to-be ex-husband's crazy with my usual brand of crazier, I just let him do what he wanted to do, knowing that karma would handle the rest. Though things never got physical, there were many times when he antagonized and emotionally provoked me, but I worked very hard to stay in integrity with my pledge to myself. I realized, after all, that we were both young, and trying to figure this relationship thing out and it was not easy. I felt an immediate shift in my energy, which made me feel lighter, happier, and more at peace. I enjoyed this feeling and vowed to work hard to keep it this way.

Things started to change immediately! The very next day, I accepted a job offer that allowed me to do work in my preferred field and location - making more money! I was so happy, and decided to move closer to Washington, D.C., to avoid such a hectic commute. That night, I found a listing in the newspaper for a rental in Alexandria City, Virginia, much closer to my new office. The older couple who owned the house were so pleasant and connected with Sydni's outgoing, two-year-old personality. They offered us their English basement apartment immediately. It was true, once I decided in my mind to change, all of these blessings came to me in the same week. I considered it a wink from God that I was on the right track, and I wanted to stay on this path. I felt so blessed and grateful and started packing immediately! Life was beginning to get good again!

Sound Scape: "Beautiful" by Snoop Dogg featuring Pharrell

#TheSydSyd circa 2005

My Discoveries & Reflections

This was a helluva life lesson for sure, one that was so painful and life-changing. I was so naïve then, I wish I'd known at that moment that what I was feeling was ok. That it was what it was and that I didn't have to explain it to anyone. I didn't know there was such a thing as honoring my feelings. I violated myself on so many levels, not listening to my internal guidance system. Once I understood what tapping into that power meant, I unapologetically stood in it and vowed to never harm myself in that way again. Be it known, that situations have come up to test my endurance on this lesson, but I have been able to choose for myself based on what I want, need, and feel.

Due to being in a loveless relationship, afraid of the restrictions being a mother would place on me, and the horrible symptoms of the Hyperemesis Gravidarum, I was on edge the majority of my pregnancy. Not only was I suffering from debilitating anxiety, the chronic throwing up zapped my energy, and to make matters worse, the general climate of fear due to the sniper shootings, only added to my angst. Unfortunately, not only had I received my hair and skin color genetically, I was an inheritor of generational trauma, unknowingly, I was now passing it down to yet another generation.

YOUR REFLECTIONS
CHAPTER 5

Discuss a time in your life when you ignored your gut-feeling and made a specific choice.

_____
_____
_____
_____
_____

What was the initial outcome?

_____
_____
_____
_____
_____

wendicherry.com   @AwakenAndHeal

What was the long-term outcome?

_____
_____
_____
_____
_____

What do you currently do when your gut is trying to tell you something?

_____
_____
_____
_____
_____

Exercise: Take a few minutes to sit still and ask for guidance on one of the situations you have been pondering over the last few weeks.

The answer may not come instantly but begin to take note of how your body feels.

When you consider the answer, does it bring you peace or a stomach ache? Don't over think it. Go towards the peace.

_____
_____
_____
_____
_____

MANTRA

I was born connected to spirit.

I can trust myself.

I love myself.

I can trust myself to know that I would never

intentionally steer myself in the wrong direction.

Chapter 6: The Goddess Awakens

"Be patient everything comes to you in the right moment."
-- Buddha

"*Happiness* can only come from inside of you and is the result of your love. When you are aware that no one else can make you happy, and that happiness is the result of your love, this becomes the greatest mastery of the Toltec: The Mastery of Love." — don Miguel Ruiz

The Mentor's Mentor and The Grasshopper

Tracy Press, President of the D.C. Chapter of the National Association of Black Female Executives in Music & Entertainment (NABFEME), had invited me to an intimate dinner with other black women in the entertainment industry. I knew the majority of the faces in the room, so I sat across from the one I didn't. She was a caramel-colored, pleasant sister who I quickly learned was a fellow Delta. In addition to being in the entertainment industry, I learned that she was a minister about to officiate the wedding of another sister sitting at the table. She was also about to donate a kidney to her cousin. "Hold up! ...who does that?" "Who is this woman?" I wondered. I came to know her as Dr. Vikki Johnson, and it became clear very quickly that she was sent by my Angels, Ancestors, and Guides to support me on my journey.

During the dinner, I told Dr. Vikki that I was engaged, so she suggested that I read a book called *The Mastery of Love* by don Miguel Ruiz. I'd never heard of him or his book but was open to checking it out. It couldn't hurt because though I was in an entirely new relationship and recently engaged, there was some unsettling in me about this relationship. Only two years in, I didn't feel like my usual silly, spontaneous, passionate self. Once my close family and friends lovingly decided to bring this to my attention, I too realized that I was not being my authentic self and was back in my old pattern of people-pleasing. Most of the time, I would not give my opinion so as not to start any arguments. Like many women, who had their noses wide-open, I had ignored several red flags in the very beginning. One of the major ones was that this person had a terrible relationship with his mother and other family members. I'd never experienced such a negative and tense relationship between a son and his mother before. Therefore, I kept my eye on the situation. As the relationship deepened, I found myself becoming more isolated, only making time to do the things he liked. He did everything he wanted to do, including hanging out with his friends every Tuesday night. It only became problematic when I tried to do the same. Even weirder, he frowned upon guests visiting our home. "Uh, oh, here we go again" I thought. The pattern of me morphing into what someone else wanted me to be was resurfacing.

Needless to say, *The Mastery of Love* book was divine intervention. Dr. Vikki suggested that we read the book as a form of premarital counseling. Thankfully, he agreed, and so every Thursday, for our couple's homework, we would sit down, read, and discuss a chapter together. This book forced me to look at my unrealistic perceptions of relationships and more importantly, my role *in* them and my expectations *of* them...and I was way off balance. It started to illuminate my constant practice of seeking love and acceptance from others instead of myself and the fact that I needed to accept and forgive myself and others for past situations. It was such an awakening! I was aware of my pattern of investing more energy into others versus myself but had never had it explained the way don Miguel broke it down in his book. We both learned lots and agreed that we needed some support to decide whether this was the right relationship for us. So, we began several months of premarital counseling and began to uncover additional red flags and cracks in our foundation and mutually decided to end our relationship. This exercise switched on a lightbulb in my head. I knew that I wanted to learn more about self-reflection and understand how the choices I'd made brought me to this station in life.

I was approaching 40-years-old and had never had a professional mentor. Up to that point, I had learned everything from Mommy, friends, and my personal experiences. But I yearned for another variety of mentor. So, after Dr. Vikki had dropped so many seeds into my lap, I began to see her as a "Mama Bird," and I was happy to be the "Baby Bird." Picture me with my mouth open wide for the next worm to nourish me. So, on my 40th birthday, I decided to give myself a gift by asking her to be my official mentor. We were both speaking on a panel for women in the entertainment industry, so afterward, I gathered up my courage and asked, "Vikki, would you be my mentor?" without a beat she said, "Sure, Grasshopper!" I was excited and though I played it cool, I was doing the Cabbage Patch dance move in my head. The Creator's timing is perfect because Vikki appeared in my life, offering support and guidance just as shit was about to get hectic!

I Was Kidnapped by the Police

"Turn around and put your hands behind your back!" the officer snarled at my mother and me. I complied, not wanting to be amongst the statistics of other melanated human beings shot dead for questioning such an absurd, unwarranted gesture. The issue was my large, copper, Wonder Woman-style bangle on my wrist, hidden under my coat. The officer was unable to see it and had little patience to try to understand why his handcuffs weren't wrapping around my wrists with ease. I was trying to explain that the bangle was the issue and that I would need to move my hands to remove it.

"Do what you want!" he spat at me. I told him I was making him clear of my next move so he wouldn't shoot me, right here, on the spot. After I removed it, he proceeded to handcuff me directly in front of my then 10-year-old daughter, who was frozen, staring at me in horror.

When my mother dropped off two bikes to get repaired, is when the fiasco began. The owner of the bike shop, Mike, had been a student of my dad's at Atlantic Highland High School in New Jersey. My dad was the first black teacher at the school in the late 60's, and with his outgoing personality, he had still made an impact on Mike all of these decades later. Mommy and Mike chatted about that for a minute, and once we realized we couldn't fit both bikes in the truck, we decided to go back the day after Thanksgiving to retrieve it. This was supposed to be a quick pit-stop en route to a post-Thanksgiving family dinner in New York. Upon arrival, Mike, the owner wasn't there but the woman who was, would not allow my mom to take the bike. She said that we could not prove that it was ours even though my mom had a tag.

I went back in to ask her the reasoning behind not allowing us to take the bikes, and she had a nasty attitude. We asked her to call Mike, and she refused. She acted like we weren't customers and kept dismissing our requests for assistance. She seemed more focused on ensuring that we could not collect this bike. So, since it was already outside on the porch and I knew what Mommy and Mike had previously agreed upon, I started to wheel the bike down to put it in the back seat of the car. As I was making my way down the ramp, I felt a tugging on the bike, then pulling on my arm. I looked up only to find the little Asian lady, dressed in a green and blue, catholic school uniform-esque skirt set. She was trying to snatch the bike from my hands. It was happening very fast, and I began chuckling to myself because I couldn't believe what was going down. Once she noticed I was determined to put this bike in the back of the truck, she began hitting me on my right side, pulling the handle-bars of the bike. I yanked it away, and she kicked me squarely in the shin with her black, patent-leather, church shoes.

I was taken aback as if the yanking and pulling wasn't enough. I was attempting to get clarity…did this chick just kick me in the shin? "Who did she think she was?" I thought to myself. After more kicking and tugging the bike handles, I swung on her, in pure self-preservation mode. Mommy was screaming, "Stop it!" and Sydni was peering from the back of the truck, eyes-wide-open. It was like a scene out of the movies.

She relented than promised to call the police. "Good, call them!" we said. That way, we can resolve this situation and continue our trip to New York. From the moment the four, yes four, police cars and two ambulances came screeching up; sirens at full volume, you would have thought we'd robbed a bank. All eight of the white police officers jumped out of their cars, one 'stood to watch' over us, and the other seven marched up the ramp to attend to the lady. Immediately I could tell that they had no interest in our side of the story.

I began taking photos of the police cars with my phone when the officer advised me to put my phone away. I asked if I had committed any crime by taking pictures, but he gruffly insisted I put the phone away. The ambulance personnel ran straight into the bike shop without checking me, Mommy, or Sydni. Mommy asked if they would monitor her blood pressure since she felt it rising. They came out to check her, and at the same time, all seven officers marched back down the ramp to tell me I was under arrest.

"Turn around and put your hands behind your back!" the officer snarled at my mother and me. Shocked, I complied though I had to very carefully make the officer aware that I needed to remove my bracelet before he could put on the cuffs. They never even read us our Miranda rights. Sydni was staring at me with her brand new, pink cell phone in her hands. She had become a texting monster since she'd only gotten her new phone two weeks prior. It had become a family joke because she would text you while she was standing right next to you. So, as they pushed me into the back of the police car, I yelled, "Call Daddy and Auntie Erinn and let them know what is happening!"

There I was, hands behind my back in the back of a damn police car. I was afraid. I remembered a clip from "The Oprah Winfrey Show", where her guest, 20-year police veteran, and expert in survival techniques with the San Diego Police Department, Sanford Strong, implored the audience, never to allow anyone to take you to another location, without alerting someone. It was at that moment that I realized that my phone was still in my coat pocket. I realized that the officers were a few yards away so, though my hands were shaking, I found a way to get my phone out of my pocket.

My first thought was to send an SOS via Facebook then changed my mind. I was in the process of interviewing for a new job and didn't want any misunderstandings. Plus, I thought people might think it was a prank so, I quickly began texting my sister, Erinn, Chers, and my Cousin George, instead. I was certain George was wondering where we were because we should have arrived at his house hours ago. This was not a joke, I hastily typed, Mommy and I were being arrested in Middletown, New Jersey. I didn't want the police officer to know that I had the phone, so I quickly put it back into my pocket. He got in the car and started to drive me to the police station. He would not allow Sydni to come with me and never even answered my inquiry about her whereabouts. They sent my mother on her way, in another police car after the EMT finished checking her.

On the drive over to the police station, my phone rang once in my pocket and miraculously answered by itself. On the other end of the phone, you could hear my cousin, George screaming in his thick, New York exit, "Yo, Cuz, where you at? What's going on?" With that, the cop barked from the front seat, "Put that phone away!"

As soon as we arrived at the police station, the officer confiscated my phone and other personal belongings. I had to take off my shoes and any other adornment. Soon after, Mommy came and they put us in a holding cell together. This was Friday, the day after Thanksgiving, after 3 p.m. This meant that we were in jeopardy of being sent to the county jail for the weekend if we were not able to get everything squared away by 5 p.m.

Eventually, they brought a crying and visibly upset Sydni to sit outside of the holding cell where Mommy and I sat in disbelief. They called me out of the cell to get mug shots and fingerprints. I remember how much trouble that cop was having trying to create my digital fingerprint. For some reason, the machine wasn't working, and he was frustrated, so he kept pinching and squeezing my fingers, trying to mold them onto the computer. Now I have seen plenty of mugshots on television, and while I was standing in front of the camera, I wondered whether or not I should smile. I know it sounds weird, but I was thinking if the story ever got out and folks started googling my mug shot, at least I'd be cute.

Luckily my sister, ex-husband, and other people became aware of what was happening. Erinn in New Jersey, Aimee in Texas and Chers, who was at a play in Manhattan, were on alert. They all started making calls to the police station to inquire about the nature of our detainment. Aimee called a family friend who worked for a local police department to investigate what was happening. He made a few calls, and since he was being given the run-around, thankfully, came to the police station to put his eyes on us. Usually, a hilarious guy, his vibe was uncharacteristically serious, which made me even more nervous. He called me over to talk to him through the bars so that he could softly explain the charges lodged against us. They were all bullshit.

Still, nobody had asked our account of the story or had taken any report from us. She claimed that *both* Mommy and I had assaulted her, which was a complete lie. They were going strictly on her word. Mommy would never have assaulted anyone. I was furious, but my friend told us to stay calm and that he'd put the police on notice. He let them know that he was keeping an eye on the situation and that they needed to clean up this mess that they had made. It took a few hours, but after a lot of calls from friends of friends, who happened to be New Jersey State Troopers, they reluctantly let us go.

This shit was expensive. I had to post bail for Mommy and me and pay a fee to get my car out of the car pound. Interestingly, they would only accept my payment in cash, which I did not have. So, I had to give Erinn my bank card and pin so she could get money from the ATM. They also refused to provide me with a receipt. I kept asking if anyone was going to record our version of the story. They said that I'd have to come back on Monday so that I could file my complaint.

The holidays were over, and we were to head back to the DMV (Washington, D.C., Maryland, Northern Virginia area) for work and school, but I stayed another night and arrived at the police station bright and early on Monday. The place was jam-packed, so I stood in the back of the long line of mostly black and brown people waiting to be seen. I was adamant that I was going to file my claim and share my side of the story.

I waited in several lines before realizing I had been in the wrong one that whole time. Then I was directed to a window where the clerk gave me a blank form. Once completed, I went back to submit the information. With a puzzled look, she told me that the specific department that I needed was closed on Mondays. The arresting officers specifically told me to come back on Monday, knowing this department would be closed, which meant they were still playing games. Before I realized it, I had tears rolling down my cheeks. I was so frustrated and furious. The woman behind the counter showed pity on me and motioned for me to follow her down the hallway. She whispered as she huddled with me in the corner and explained my only other option was to come back the next day. I told her that I didn't even live in New Jersey and needed to get back home. I thanked her and walked out.

Just as I was walking back to my car, I checked my email and saw a Google alert for my name. I'd placed a Google alert on my name years prior, to make me aware of the mention of my name in the media. I couldn't believe it, we had already been put in the local police blotter for three different cities in the county. It gave our ages, home addresses, and it said that we were under arrest for simple assault. At least they reduced the charges, but it was still all a lie.

The typical narrative is that police harass only melanated men. However, on this day, I realized any melanated human being was at risk. There was no reason for them to treat us the way that they did.

We were tax-paying citizens who deserved, at the very least, some courtesy from those sworn to protect and serve.

Mommy was nervous about what people would say, but I didn't give a shit what those local yokels thought. Anyone who cared about us would not assume we committed this crime and would have the decency to ask what had happened before making a snap judgment. Soon letters from the court started flowing in for several upcoming court dates. With help from one of my Delta Sorors, I secured a lawyer and began to tell him the story. It took thousands of dollars and lots of time trying to document what had happened. Four months later, Mommy's case was closed, but they wanted to put the charges on my permanent record. I told them I was willing to fight it, and the owner of the bike store finally settled it.

I felt like I was caught in the matrix because every day, there was an account on the news of someone else being harassed, arrested, or killed, just for the color of their skin. A friend asked me to share my story along with a group of other people with similar experiences for a short film. However, they could not use the footage because the other people got cold feet for fear of some backlash from work, family, or the community. The news saddened me and was very disappointing. These stories were worth sharing, but the other subjects of this film didn't feel safe sharing their truth about their mistreatment by the police. I was angry. In my opinion, the only reason things worked in my favor was that I had the resources to secure a lawyer to fight on our behalf. What about the other melanated people who don't have the money, the connections, and the resolve to ensure fair treatment. My perspective on life, the judicial system, and my safety changed forever after that experience.

Love or Fear – Choose One

"You have to choose one, either love or fear," is what Dr. Vikki told me after this traumatic experience. "Are those really my only choices?", I wondered. I wasn't convinced, it all seemed too simple. I wasn't feeling fear or love, just anger, and disgust. What was there to love about what had unjustly happened to Mommy and Me?

A few months later, Dr. Vikki invited me to her home for an invite-only event.

The invitation read:

June 6, 2012

Dear Butterfly,

"Imagine this...joining a powerful, spirit-filled room full of amazing women in launching the best days of your life. If you ever experience procrastination, worry, anxiety, doubt, hesitation, stress, tension...then join me in The Fearless Success Salon. If you are ready to move into your harvest season and reap the blessings and wealth that has been set aside for you, then you will want to be a part of this special gathering at my home.

You will learn to:

- *Manifest the power of all that has been placed within you boldly and powerfully.*
- *Identify what has been standing in the way of moving forward.*
- *Recognize and eliminate fear from your mindset, spirit, and business.*
- *Understand the truth about fear and how to apply this revelation.*

*If you are serious about eliminating fear from your life (even your hidden fears) then **RSVP**. I'd love to have you there. **This is non-transferable and by invitation only, please.***

Have a powerful day,

Vikki

Intriguing, right?! When was the last time you got an invitation offering such promises as that? On the real, I'd already had plans for that day but canceled them immediately because I knew that an invitation of this type to her home was a big deal. Once I arrived, though I didn't know anyone else, I still felt the palatable energy of excitement, anticipation, and gratitude for having been invited. We opened with prayer, and Dr. Vikki shared that in her leadership position, she often ran in the same circles and that she was ready to pass down many of the empowering lessons she'd learned over the years. Even better, she had identified *us* as women who she and her co-presenter were willing to pour into and support as we ascended to the next level in our spiritual and professional lives.

We learned that identifying and releasing fear was a significant step in evolving into the next generation of powerful women, unapologetically, and fearlessly, dominating in business and life.

One of the most profound exercises was when she asked us to write down what percentage of our day was spent doing the things that we felt aligned with our purpose. After thinking about it for a few minutes, I figured I'd better be honest so, I wrote 35 percent. I was almost embarrassed to share that with the other ladies that I wasn't clear on my purpose. I mean, from the outside, my job looked terrific; however, in my heart, I was simply there taking Dr. Vikki's advice to "*water my garden and get my check.*" I had spent so many years supporting the careers and passions of others that I'd completely neglected my own. I had recently begun to explore the things that really excited me but still wasn't clear on what type of flowers I wanted in my garden. Even though I was making more money than any other job, it didn't constitute pure joy. The question was, what would bring me pure joy?

On the second card, we were to write what our name would be if we were working on our purpose at 100 percent. I thought for a while but kept drawing a blank. I didn't even know what she was talking about and was too nervous to ask any questions. Luckily another attendee asked the clarifying questions. In a soothing voice, Dr. Vikki simply asked us to get quiet, close our eyes, still our minds, and ask God for the answer. The room became peaceful and contemplative; I had my eyes closed, but it was taking everything within me not to pop one eye-ball open to see what everyone else was doing. "Am I slow?" I questioned myself. Nothing was coming, and I wasn't sure how much time we had to figure this out - which made me more anxious. I was beginning to think this information may be too deep for me; I didn't want to end up being the only clueless and nameless one.

Just at that moment, a voice came into my head clear as a bell. "Core...Cora...Cora...," the sound played over and over in my head. Cora?! "What is the significance of that?" I wondered. It was clear that I wanted to learn more about myself, specifically more about my biological influences. I was trying to get to the "core" of who I was. It was as if a light bulb had gone off in my head. Cora...it made sense to me. I started to feel the emotion welling up inside of me but didn't want to embarrass myself by bursting into tears in front of everyone so, I gathered myself and ran into the bathroom and had a mini-meltdown, not in a negative way but in a positive way. I sobbed because, at that moment, it made sense to me that I was *not* working at 100 percent. Now the real work had to begin to figure out what that 100 percent was.

All of those years later, the desire to create a deeper connection within myself related to my birth family had only exacerbated. You see, my girl in my head, Oprah, had just been "found" by a biological half-sister, that she never knew existed. I must have re-watched that episode one million times; it was so heartwarming, emotional, and intriguing to watch. I was determined to follow my instinct and desire to find out more about who I was at my core – spiritually, emotionally, and physically.

My friend Jawanza told me that in African culture, Cora would be spelled with a 'K.' I became fascinated to learn more about the name Kora. After more research, I realized that technically, a 'Kora' was an instrument first used in Gambia, West Africa, a hybrid of a harp, a Spanish guitar, and a lute with 21-strings. The players of this traditional instrument were usually the Jalis (griots), traditional historians, genealogists, and storytellers whose mission it was to transmit the history of families and their land generation after generation.[14] The connection to the Kora at this particular time felt like a cruel joke. Up to that point, I hadn't had any communication with my biologicals in years, but it wasn't for lack of trying…at least on my part.

Thankfully, as the years passed, Dr. Vikki would gently and strategically drop another seed of wisdom, concept, or consideration, into my lap that would propel my life on a quantum leap forward. One day she sent a text that simply read, "Do you want to change your life?" I wrote back, "Yup!" Then she sent a link to a movie called "Hidden Colors." "Hidden Colors" was a documentary about the untold history of people of color around the globe that discusses some of the reasons the contributions of African and aboriginal people were hidden from history. I'd always been interested in history, but not the kind taught in traditional schools. I was disgusted by what I came to learn from this documentary and began to see race relations, the plight of melanated people from an entirely new lens. It wasn't totally foreign because during my youth, a seed had been planted in my mind about the power and brilliance of melanated people. I'd grown up with members of The Nation of Gods and Earths who teach that Black people are the original people of the planet Earth, and therefore they are the fathers ("Gods") and mothers ("Earths") of civilization.[15] So, the concepts weren't as far-off as I remembered from my school days.

With this new sense of curiosity, I became a sponge, slowly but surely peeling back the layers of having lived with such a closed mind for so long. I asked The Creator to show me the *'truth'*, in whatever form, just as long as it was the truth. Well, the old adage, you get what you ask for is true because I attracted all types of lessons, messages, revelations, people, and new (to me) information. I began reading books from 'Master Teachers' like Dr. Yosef Ben Jochanan, Dr. John Henrik Clarke, Anthony Browder, Dr. Francis Cress Welsing, and many more. I fell wholeheartedly and gratefully down the rabbit hole, absorbing all of this knowledge. It was partly overwhelming, exhilarating, exciting, saddening, and opened my eyes to see myself differently.

Some of these new concepts, ideas, and theories had been on my radar over the years, but I didn't rock the boat by asking questions. I *was* a sheep for sure, simply boxing myself into a value system that was no longer serving my needs, to be liked or accepted.

This awakening, coupled with my anger at having been arrested and the constant killing of melanated bodies, was becoming too much. Up to that point, I'd attended one of the more popular churches in Alexandria, Virginia. It was led by a handsome, charismatic, young pastor from the mid-west, who was very influential in the D.C. Metro area. He had a touch of swag, the gift of gab, and the unique ability to work with his large, multi-generational congregation. I'd been a committed member, engrossing myself and my daughter in the plethora of activities and opportunities this well-heeled organization provided. That was until after I was arrested, and the suggestion by the church's leadership to rely on praying versus taking action raised both my eyebrows and blood pressure.

I was exhausted from being asked to hold on until Jesus came back to save me. Chile. I was now clear, and there was no need to give my power over to a spiritual system whose figurehead didn't look like me or any of my ancestors. One that had historically (and currently) suppressed melanated people and wielded the power of judgment like a sledgehammer. Within this system, I felt stifled, unfulfilled, timid, and constantly afraid of making the wrong moves for fear of being "struck down". The freedom that came with liberating myself from my bondage AND the bondage of this spiritual system, six-years later, is still hard to describe.

I had never felt so many emotions at one time. What was 100 percent clear was that I had been had, hood-winked, bamboozled, and conditioned to believe many of these concepts which had been proven to be flat out lies. I felt sort of like when I realized there was no Santa Clause. Once the ole' Santa mythology was exposed, Mommy told me she was glad the lie was over because for years she was mad that some old, fat, white dude had gotten all of the credit for her hard work each Christmas. In my opinion, these lies were created to keep melanated people from remembering their power, and not only their power but from rising to stand once-and-for-all.

To stand against the injustices inflicted upon them since the colonizing of the United States. To keep them docile and humble, waiting for the 'after-life' to fully enjoy themselves. It took a few years to absorb the information, re-program my brain, and to decipher how I wanted to apply it to my personal life. One thing was clear; I was pure God/dess power, in human form.

I disengaged from the activities that had previously commanded so much of my time. I retreated into my lab to study, create, awaken, heal, plot, and activate. I was very stealthy about it. Honestly, I didn't need permission from anyone; I wasn't looking for any nods of approval from any specific groups of people, I followed my intuition and what felt peaceful to me at that time. I mean, seriously, you can't tell everyone that you read a few books and decided to change the trajectory of your life, and not expect some serious side-eyes.

Without even knowing it, I was just one of the hundreds of melanated women nationwide who were questioning traditional Christianity, and I became immersed in ancient African spirituality, symbolism, and culture.[16] I decided to use the brain, wisdom, and intellect The Creator gave me to unzip and step out of my sheep suit. I stood proudly in the notion that I was not born a worm, unworthy, less than, unable to enjoy my life until I made it to 'the-sweet-by-and-by' aka heaven. Hell no! Over and over again, my studies proved to me, that I was born pure love, with the God/dess-power already within me. I came to the planet, at this specific time, to co-create an amazing life. My birthright was good health, pleasure, money, abundance, fun, joy, peace, in the here and now.

As I was expanding my knowledge of spirituality, my health was still a challenge. In addition to the fibroids, I'd experienced numbness in my fingers and toes and was tested for Multiple Sclerosis by a neurologist. Lyme's Disease and Bell's Palsy had already been ruled out as the root cause of the persistent, electric shock-like pain deep inside of my ear. That pain was indescribable at times, and it was only after visits to an oral surgeon, an otolaryngologist (ear, nose, and throat), and suffering through an MRI, with my severe claustrophobia, that my last resort was the neurologist. One of the tests, unbeknownst to me, was for her to shock me 40 times, 20 times in each leg with an electrical instrument. I hadn't been prepped or warned about the pain of this test because most people refuse it if forewarned.

So, there I was, sitting on the table like a sacrificial lamb when the first painful shock in the back of my leg sent an electric surge throughout my body. "What the...?" I exclaimed but in more colorful language. "What type of test is this?" I queried, in my outside voice. She lied when she assured me it was almost over because I had no idea that I was in for another 39 shocks. I was in tears and traumatized by the end of the procedure, she was right, had I known about the severity of this test, I never would have agreed. After all of those tests, doctor's bills, appointments, and pain, not one single doctor was able to tell me the cause of that lightning bolt sensation deep within my ear.

One month later, Dr. Vikki invited me to her *Girl Talk Unplugged – The Ultimate Getaway Retreat* in Cambridge, Md. The keynote speaker was a petite, African woman named Dr. Sakiliba Mines, the medical director of The Institute of Multidimensional Medicine in Washington, D.C. Though small in stature, she got on that stage and transformed into a powerhouse. After a quick introduction, she got right to the hard questions, ones that I had never even considered before. She was moving quickly, pacing back and forth across the stage, asking:

"Do you drink water?"

"Do you cook your own food?"

"Do you get enough sunshine on your skin?"

The most profound question that shook me out of my slumber was...

"Do you love yourself?"

"Well, do you?" I asked myself silently.

It only took me a few minutes, but I started to realize that the answer to all of her questions was a resounding - NO! By the end of her speech, I was intrigued. I knew that I needed to schedule an appointment with her, stat! On my first visit, which lasted two hours, she asked me some of those same questions and then more impactful ones. She asked about the time I went to sleep, my diet, whether or not I exercised, and how I managed my stress? Initially, I couldn't even answer all of those questions because I didn't know. It felt like she wanted to get to know me and honestly, I wasn't that in-tune with myself up to that point. Life was hectic. I was assuming a new role in my career, being a single mom who was trying to eke out some sort of social life, while on the tail-end of a relationship. I was frequently emotional, physically, and spiritually exhausted; I knew that I was not taking the best care of myself. Though she didn't take insurance, I vowed to make an appointment with her ASAP.

No More Cutting

I used to hate my body. My seventh-grade boyfriend was the first to ever plant the seed that there may be something 'wrong' when he announced to the entire after school bus that I was a 25-25-25, versus the mythological 36-24-36, that we saw on TV. There were a few chuckles, but I honestly didn't even know what it meant. After that statement, I became obsessed with the things that I did not like about my body. I was not athletic and began to compare myself to all of the other girls, especially in high school. By the time I'd gotten to college, I was in full self-hate mode. By spring break my freshman year, I realized that I needed new bras. All of my tops were becoming too tight, and I was spilling over the C cup bra, the size I'd worn for years. Up to that point, I'd never paid attention to my breast size. It was uncomfortable and embarrassing, so I noticed that I began folding my arms over my breasts as a way to camouflage them. That was the beginning of more than a decade of being insecure. I was thin, with a small frame, and began to experience minor back pain, and the bra straps would dig into my shoulders. Every time I went to get measured for a bra, the size would have increased, which altered the proportion of my body, increasing my negative body image. I vowed that someday I would get a cosmetic breast reduction.

It took me 22 years, but I finally saved up enough money and found who I thought was the right doctor to perform the surgery. After three consultations with this doctor, I was excited to move forward. I felt confident because I had researched the procedure for the past ten years and had saved up enough to pay for the entire procedure in cash. The surgeon seemed to understand my vision, and I was ready to move forward. I also shared my concerns and feelings with the person I was seeing at the time, and though he understood, he was not happy about me having an elective surgical procedure. I reassured him that everything would be fine.

After my breast reduction surgery, I was so excited to begin trying on all of the clothes that I had saved to wear over the years. Oddly, the clothes weren't fitting as I'd envisioned. After the period where the swelling was supposed to have gone down, I realized that not only had my breast size not decreased, it had increased. After a few months post-surgery, I couldn't believe that I'd spent all of those years saving up all of that money only for the doctor to not perform the surgery as we'd agreed. I was so upset that I had visions of going to his office to physically fist-fight him and for a short amount of time, became depressed. In the end, I'd flushed thousands of dollars down the proverbial drain.

I was only a few months post-op when I had my first appointment with Dr. Mines. She required an in-depth health and surgery history, a list of all of my medicines and supplements, and a food diary. She asked the most intriguing questions, ones that my doctor had never asked me in the 10-years I'd been her patient. Though I was utterly embarrassed, I had to tell her about my recently botched cosmetic surgery, three fibroid surgeries, and tubal ligation. She listened intently and asked me why I'd gone through with such invasive procedures. I gave her my reasons for each that I felt my body was not proportioned, my breasts made me feel subconscious, and that over the years, I began experiencing minor back pain. I explained that my gynecologist had suggested those three fibroid removal procedures, and most importantly, I didn't want any more children or Hyperemesis Gravidarum again so, tubal ligation seemed like the only option. Dr. Mines listened intently, then without blinking, she looked directly in my eyes and in a soft but firm voice said, "Ms. Cherry…NO MORE CUTTING!"

I was ashamed and had an epiphany at that moment that I needed to love myself as I was. That there was nothing, I should be doing to try to change myself. That was easy to say because after years of negative messages from outsiders, I had to own the most harmful ones that came from my mind. It took some work to re-program my mind to be okay with what I saw in the mirror.

For the next few months, Dr. Mines suggested an elimination diet, which included no grains (I love pancakes) or dairy (yes, that included my kryptonite, pizza!). It was also suggested that I increase my fruit and vegetable intake, exercise more, drink more water, eat my last meal by 7 p.m. and hit the hay by 10 p.m. That was a tall order, but after so many years of suffering, I was desperate to give it a try. She also suggested a few supplements to bring my levels back to normal after she reviewed my blood tests. One of the most intriguing prescriptions was to add the ancient practice of colon hydrotherapy, infrared sauna, and an Aqua Chi Foot Bath to boot.[17] After a few months, I lost seven pounds; my skin began to glow, I had more energy, my bloating went down, and voila - no more numbness. It was the grains the entire time. My blood test revealed that I had a celiac sensitivity, which meant I was allergic to wheat, grains, and flour. I still had the fibroids but felt so energetic and renewed. I was onto something, and my excitement was building, things were changing around these parts – I wanted to tell everyone!

Thema's Pot

Like E.F. Hutton, when Dr. Vikki spoke, I *mostly* listened. I told her that I was *still* struggling with fibroids, even after three surgeries so, she introduced me to yet another powerhouse named Thema Azize Serwa, the visionary of The Womb Sauna.[18] In my many years of fibroid research, I had never heard of the ancient practice of Yoni Steaming (vaginal steaming) before but according to Thema, Yoni is a Sanskrit word meaning 'vagina', 'womb' and 'origin of life', and represents the goddess Shakti, the creative force that moves through the entire universe. Yoni Steaming is intended to support, nurture, and heal the divine feminine, physically, emotionally, and spiritually plus a wide-range of menstrual and reproductive issues.

Prince died on the morning of my first Womb Sauna appointment. I was already full of nervous energy, in anticipation of sitting on the pot for the first time, and this news exacerbated my emotions. I'd arrived early and sat in the car, listening to all of the Prince songs and sad reflections flooding the airways. I was in denial because I honestly hadn't gotten over Michael's (Jackson) passing. Once they played my favorite song, "Adore" I realized it was true and a few tears slid down my cheeks.

Thankfully, the Womb Sauna experience was relaxing and enlightening as she placed me on a steaming pot of herbs, sat at my feet, and began to ask me the most profound yet simple questions. "Do you know how powerful you are?" "Who, Moi?" I looked at her like she had two heads. She told me that I was playing small and that I had more power within me than I knew. She shared that I was choosing to live the life that I was living at this point, and after a quick balancing exercise, pointed out that I had an excess of masculine energy. Who knew? Certainly not me…I'd never heard of this concept, but it made sense. I was a single mom, in a leadership position at work, and had watched my single mom gracefully handle her business my entire life. That, coupled with my 20+ plus years of event production and logistics experience, I was used to getting shit done. Sitting on the pot that day not only allowed the steam from the herbs to rise and permeate my girlie parts, but it was penetrating my heart and soul. It was encouraging me to see myself in a fresh, more empowered light. I realized that my fibroids had been a gift to push me to be more creative, out of my complacency, and to tap into my own Divine Feminine Goddess power.

Getting on "Thema's pot" became a regular part of my new and much-needed self-care ritual. She introduced me to and permitted me to tap into my sensual and sexual energy. Something that my former spiritual practice forbade. I began to meditate on the life that I wanted and decided not to dwell on what was causing me misery. Over the next few months, I took her six-week Womb Intensive Healing course and learned so much about the energetic causes of fibroids and how I may have attracted them ancestrally, with my past behaviors, and traumas. I had no idea that this was 'a thing.' Not one of my "highly educated" doctors or surgeons even remotely offered me such information. Thema was the first person to talk to me about radical self-love and how it needed to be a key component of my healing journey.

With more intense research, I came to learn that in women, the Sacral Chakra was the seat of all of my creativity or lack thereof. Remember, since the 7th grade, I'd told myself that I was not creative, so in essence, I had stifled that part of myself very early on. From the Sacral Chakra, women are either birthing a baby, business, idea, or concept.[19] It was also where I'd been holding on to the pains of failed relationships, my abortions, and feelings of not being safe. The Sacral Chakra is also called the "dwelling place of the Self," according to intuitive healer Anarah, based out of Laguna Beach in California, this chakra influences not only partnership and relationships but also our grounded-ness in our own identity, our ability to set boundaries and maintain our personal space. Bingo! Sounds familiar, right? I'd struggled with boundaries, personal space, partnerships, and relationships for the majority of my 20's and 30's.

Let me break this down for the people in the back...the word *Chakra* is a Sanskrit (an ancient Indic language) word that translates to a wheel or disk. In yoga, meditation, and Ayurveda (Ayurveda is a science of life (*Ayur* = life, *Veda* = science or knowledge). It offers a body of wisdom designed to help people stay vibrant and healthy while realizing their full human potential.[20] This term refers to wheels of energy throughout the body. There are seven main chakras, which align the spine, starting from the base of the spine through to the crown of the head. To visualize a chakra in the body, imagine a swirling wheel of energy where matter and consciousness meet, according to Michelle Fondin, Vedic Educator at the (Deepak) Chopra Center.[21]

Unfortunately, in the melanated community, women especially, suffer more than any other population in the U.S. from poor health outcomes. The rate of postpartum mortality, regardless of socioeconomic status or education level, is the highest in the nation. Also, more than 80 percent of African-American women have developed fibroids by the time they're 50-years-old. Many fibroids go undetected unless they cause symptoms. Uterine fibroids (medically known as uterine leiomyomata) are common, non-cancerous (benign) tumors of the uterus consisting of smooth muscle cells and connective tissue. A woman may have one fibroid or groups of several fibroids. [22] This coupled with our desire to be the mythological Superwoman on the daily, low-grade stressors, poor diets, lack of rest, and exercise, mixed with our addiction to sugar, are some of our most dangerous killers.

It was all starting to make sense now. My health issues were part of a much larger problem of lifestyle choices, epigenetics, nature vs. nurture, my environment, food choices, and the like...I was both enlightened and enraged. It doesn't help that melanated women were often unseen and unheard of in the Western medical establishment. I remember doctors looking at me like I was crazy when I continued to tell them something didn't feel right, and my pain was persisting, even though I'd followed their protocols "to-the-t." I, like everyone else, had been trained to believe everything the doctors said because I felt uncomfortable asking clarifying questions, even when I didn't truly understand a diagnosis. I fired my doctor of 10-years with the quickness once I experienced the level of care an integrative doctor like Dr. Mines provided for me.

The Zen Palace: Writing the Vision

On one of my visits to sit on Thema's pot, I told her that I wanted to buy a house. She asked me to describe the type of house I wanted. Honestly, I had no clue so she instructed me to visualize what my dream home would look like, to get clear on the number of rooms, what the walls looked like, and how I wanted the environment to feel. I was confident that I wanted lots of natural sunlight, lots of space, and at least two full bathrooms. I needed space for an office and an eat-in kitchen. That night I wrote it all down in my journal, and over the next few months, I started my home buying process.

My realtor took me to places that he thought would be in my budget. I told him that it was clear that I was going to get what I wanted, so to not waste my time going to places that didn't meet my criteria. I wanted what I wanted and after sitting on that pot a few more times, knowing that I deserved it. Finally, I had a contract on a particular unit and was waiting to hear if the seller accepted my offer.

My eyes popped open at 4 a.m. that morning, and spirit instantly told me to browse the Redfin website. Voilà, the first property that popped up was in the same building, the same floor plan and square footage as the one I'd had on contract, but it was $30,000 less. Wow! How could this be? I immediately emailed my realtor and sent him the link so that in the morning, my email would be at the top of his inbox. In my excitement, I had trouble getting back to sleep, but when I finally woke up to check my email, he told me that my bid hadn't been accepted anyway so, he'd scheduled a viewing for us at the new one at 6 p.m. that night.

Sydni and I met the 90-year old owner of the well-kept and decorated unit. She was moving to an assisted living facility and had taken great care of the unit over the past 40-years. It was awesome to walk around and visualize it as my own home. After a few weeks of back-and-forth, I signed my name on the dotted line and had the keys in my hand for a great interest rate. I was so excited, and I have Thema to thank for helping me be clear with the universe about my vision and to myself.

Kat and The Red Tent

The adage says, "When the student is ready, the teacher will appear..." It's true in my experience. My Sorority Sister, Kayenecha, was the first person to hip me to the gatherings of the Ladies of the Red Tent. They were run by a local, young Nigerian woman named, Risikat 'Kat' Okedeyi of Lil SoSo Productions. I was intrigued by the time I hit the door. We were all invited to bring a snack and a pillow. Upon arrival, we began to gather in a circle in the center of the room. The mood in the room and amongst the other melanated sisters, many of them I didn't know, was easy-going, welcoming, refreshing, authentic, and warm. Before we began to share, there were a few rituals that were performed that I was not accustomed to, like the reading of Tarot cards. At that moment, I still held rigorous thoughts and feelings connected with my spiritual system so, some of the information I absorbed and some of it I didn't. I don't remember the topic of discussion that particular night - only that I was intrigued and felt so empowered and connected when I left that room. I was excited to learn more and felt safe enough in this space, with these specific women, to explore more of these rituals they seemed to enjoy. I rarely missed a gathering of the Red Tent over the next year and was grateful for the way Kat presented the information in such an easy to digest and judgment-free format.

During each gathering, Kat presented a relevant topic of discussion, and I'd become so fascinated, I invited a few friends to join me in this soul and eye-opening experience. On one occasion, I told Kat that I kept waking up at 5:37 a.m. every morning. It just didn't make sense to me, but like clockwork, every day, I'd open my eyes, check the clock, and boom - it would be 5:37 a.m. - on the dot! So, she looked up the meaning in a numerology book; now, at that time, I hadn't had any significant exposure to this type of esoteric information. As far as I had been taught, numerology was 'of the devil.' She read aloud from the book the meaning of the number '5-3-7', it read:

"The ascended masters congratulate you on the changes you're making, as they are putting you squarely on the right path."

I instantly broke into tears; that didn't sound evil to me. Luckily Chers, was there to offer me a tissue and a hug. My heart was full because I'd been becoming increasingly conflicted about my spiritual life, and knowing I was on the right path gave me the push I needed to continue my exploration.

Some of the doctrines I'd raised myself with, I'd already been side-eyeing. You see, Mommy was not a church-goer so, the majority of my exposure to church was from Grandmommy and Granddaddy on the Eastern Shore. I'd made church-going a regular practice throughout college and into my early 40s, but now I was questioning lots of things and with the revelation that I was on the right path – I was more inspired to be open to what I was learning at the Red Tent gatherings, through the 'Master Teachers' and the new revelations about myself.

From the moment one of my favorite Soul Mates shared Outkast's song "Liberation" with me, it instantly resonated deeply within my spirit. It saw this song as a message for me to release myself from years of self-hatred and the fear of rejection. Though it had taken many years for me to get to this point, I was finally ready for the liberation of my mind, body, and spirit.

"There's a fine line between love and hate you see…"
"Came way too late, but baby I'm on it…"

"Can't worry bout, what a nigga think now see…"
"That's Liberation and baby I want it…"

"Shake that load off, shake that load off…"

"Shake that load off, shake that load off…"

Sound Scape: "Liberation" by Outkast

Awakening
(Photo: Derrick Watkins, 2012)

My Discoveries & Reflections

Spirituality

It is the right of every person to experience their own spiritual journey without judgement or pressure to conform to society's standards. Do what works for you without attempting to proselytize others. (Def. To convert someone from one religion, belief, or opinion to another.)

Guides

Chapter six marked the beginning of my true awakening and healing. There were so many profound lessons, I'd attracted so many powerful guides into my life. It was both overwhelming and exhilarating. The tipping point for me was being detained. Your aha moment could be something entirely different; the point is that you've decided to explore. The process looks different for everyone.

There should be no judgment for where any one person is in their process. As you evolve personally, you must be gentle and kind to yourself. This work can be challenging. For many of us, we may be the first people in our family to explore a new horizon. The information we learn, the new ideas we intend to investigate, may be worlds away from what we were taught, or how we were raised. It is ok if others don't understand.

Over the years, each generation has used the tools and information they had at the time to support them. However, times change and what worked for past generations may not work for you in this modern era. Give yourself permission to think new thoughts and be open to other points-of-view. Look for like-minded people to support your exploration. I was so blessed to have attracted these guides who intentionally and by osmosis supported and encouraged my evolution. A few of these women I have never met in person but still have been impacted by their message.

Epigenetics

Thema's 6-Week Womb Healing Intensive program, opened my eyes to the fact that I could heal my womb. Some of the anxiety I was carrying was transgenerational trauma, and with the right support, my womb would heal. It is true that we share our parents' genetic makeup, however, according to Dr. Deepak Chopra, one of Oprah's faves and co-author of *Super Genes: Unlock the Astonishing Power of Your DNA for Optimum Health and Well-Being*.[23] 'Epigenetics' claims that only 5 percent of our DNA makeup is genetically connected to our family. The other 95 percent is lifestyle-related. Simply put, our long-term vitality is determined by how well *we* manage stress, the types of food we put into our bodies, the frequency of our exercise regimen, and most importantly, our level of emotional and environmental toxicity. The wonderful news is that we—not our family makeup—have the power to ensure our wellness and stave off lifestyle-related diseases.

YOUR REFLECTIONS
CHAPTER 6

What value system do you subscribe to?

_____

_____

_____

Why that one in particular?

_____

_____

_____

_____

_____

Is it one that you believe in or one that was passed down to you
from your family?

_____

_____

_____

_____

_____

wendicherry.com   @AwakenAndHeal

What diseases have you been told "run in your family"?
Do you have said disease?

_____

_____

_____

_____

_____

Have you ever considered that you have control over 95 percent
of what happens to your body according to the science of
epigenetics?

That means based on the type of food you eat, the amount of
daily rest and exercise you get, how you process stress and your
environment all play a role in dis-ease in the body.

_____

_____

_____

_____

How do you feel about this theory?
Are you open to exploring more integrative (mind, body, spirit)
modalities of healing versus the "Western" standard of care?

_____

_____

_____

_____

Chapter 7: Wandering Wendi

"We've Been Waiting for You!" – The Ancestors

On my 37th birthday, I received an AfricanAncestry.com DNA test as a gift. A simple swab of the cells in my cheeks would allow me to trace my birth mother's, mother's, mother's, mother's, maternal line back to its origin. As a woman, I could only trace the X chromosome on my family tree, whereas males can test both the X (maternal) and Y (paternal) chromosomes. I assumed it would be on the continent of Africa but anxiously awaited the results for confirmation. The DNA testing was a new technology at that time, and since I'd still had no contact with my biological family, I felt it was the only way I could learn more about my genetic roots. Watching the shows, "Who Do You Think You Are" and "Finding Your Roots" with Skip Gates, inspired me to continue my search to find out who I was. Admittedly, I used to hate on the families who were able to make connections but always held out hope that my day would come.

On December 20, 2007, I returned home from my father's funeral on the Eastern Shore of Maryland to find an envelope from AfricanAncestry.com on my bed. I excitedly opened it to reveal that I was from the Mafa people living in the Extreme North Region of Cameroon. Cameroon? Mafa Tribe? What the heck does this all mean? It was both overwhelming and intriguing. I jumped on Google for more information, but to my disappointment, there was not much there so, though I could finally identify an actual spot on the continent, I felt no real connection to Cameroon. I did, however, feel like I was closing that chapter of my life by burying my father that day and opening a fresh, new chapter, one that was connected to my biological family. I was excited to have the Cameroonian connection but still desired a link to the family living right there in New Jersey. It would be many more years until I was able to set foot on the Mother Land.

By 2012, Erinn and I had reconnected with our biological family. During that time, I shared my DNA results along our ancestral maternal line. The results encompassed my birth mother, grandmother, great grandmother, and my sisters, brothers, maternal aunts, uncles, nieces, nephews, cousins, even Sydni, and her future children. Now I wanted to know more about the Paternal side of my family tree. However, only men carry a Y chromosome, so women cannot take the PatriClan Test.[24] The only way for a woman to trace her paternal lineage is to have a male relative from her father's side take the test. With that knowledge, I convinced my biological father to test his mother's lineage using the African Ancestry MatriClan DNA test, with a simple swab of the cheek. It revealed our Paternal ancestral Grandmother was from the Temne ethnic group in Sierra Leone, Africa, by 99.7 percent.

In February 2015, at a screening of BET Network's the "Book of Negroes," a story of a kidnapped Sierra Leonian woman who attempted to secure her freedom in the eighteenth century, I felt compelled to visit Africa as soon as possible. As the credits rolled, I randomly blurted out to my friend Janaye Ingram, that I was going to Cameroon. I didn't have any set travel plans; it was just on my bucket list. She said, "I am, too, when are you going?" I explained that it just came out of my mouth and that I didn't have any idea. "Well, I'm going in October!" she said. I immediately asked if I could join her and the very next day she introduced me to Raoul Keddy, Founder & Managing Director, Raked International, LLC, who had extended her an invitation to speak at the African-America Business Summit. She told him that I had traced my DNA back to Cameroon and to my great surprise, he invited me along. My only expense was my airfare because he was going to take care of my ground transportation, hotel, and food. I could hardly contain my excitement! I was finally Cameroon-bound! Timing is everything, and slowly but surely, I believe my Ancestors began orchestrating the people, resources, and opportunities for me to learn more about this "far off" land and my people. "It's time; we've been waiting for you...", I imagined them saying.

Around that same time, the Co-Founder and President of African Ancestry, Gina Paige, introduced me to Ambassador Joseph Charles Bienvenu Foe-Atangana, the former Ambassador of the Republic of Cameroon. He invited us to his official residence on Embassy Row in Washington, D.C., and I found his family, and staff to be warm and welcoming. On our first visit, Ambassador Feo shared some historical and spiritual lessons on the origins of the Mafa people in the Extreme North. Soon, Sydni and I became frequent guests to the residence for Sunday dinners with his wife, children, and grandchildren. Dishes included traditional Cameroonian fare like Ndole, a spinach stew made with bitter leaves, plantains, and accra bananas. It felt like the family dinners on the movie *Soul Food,* everyone gathering to enjoy good food, music, and company.

It was interesting to see this multigenerational family speaking a blend of languages, including their Pidgen mixed with French and English, both of which are considered official languages used by the government of Cameroon. I tried my best to keep up with what was being asked, but it still provided a bit of a language barrier for us. The ability to speak multiple languages is a gift and made me wish I hadn't been slacking off in the back row of my seventh-grade Spanish class. However, I was grateful that I had the foresight to enroll Sydni in a Spanish Immersion program for seven years to make her a multi-lingual, global citizen. This experience with the Ambassador and his family gave us a unique and intimate level of exposure to how a family from Cameroon enjoys life. I enjoyed taking note of the differences and similarities between this and the families I knew in the US. One thing was clear, they had a lot of pride in their country, traditions, music, and food, and it just made me more grateful to have been allowed to have a glimpse into my new-found Cameroonian culture.

While attempting to learn as much as I could about the country called "Africa in Miniature" before my trip, I learned that Cameroon has – an active volcanic mountain, lush jungles, white and black sand beaches, a myriad of wildlife, historical sites, and diverse cultural backgrounds.[25]

Also, the Islamic invasion of the 1700's and the Christian invasion of the 19th century displaced most of the indigenous peoples. By 1884, Germany had colonized the country even further, stripping them of their resources, language, spiritual system, and land by forcing their languages and euro-centric customs upon them. It was both an eye-opening and angering experience for me that a group of people would have the audacity to inflict such trauma on another group of people. I became even more committed to learning as much as I could about my country and my people. I was itching to put my feet in the soil.

Honoring the Ancestors

In March 2015, I attended the memorial ceremony for Dr. Yosef ben Jochannan,[26] considered one of the more prominent Afrocentric scholars, writers, and historians. I was fascinated to see that an organization named The African Diaspora Ancestral Commemoration Institute (ADACI) had created an ancestral altar in his honor. This was unlike any altar I'd ever seen before. I was vaguely familiar with ancestral altars from Kat's teachings in the Red Tent, but Eurica Huggins-Axom described the tradition and the elements of this particular alter to the attendees at the ceremony. There were photos of other luminaries who had already passed into

147

the ancestral realm, tea lights, candles, fruit, and the Sankofa symbol which, is a West African Adinkra symbol, representing the act of going back and fetching wisdom. According to her organization, "In the African tradition, the altar is a physical area where we venerate (honor) the ancestors and which serves as a focal point to express feelings and emotions within a sacred space." [27]

She encouraged us to call out the names of our ancestors, and someone poured libations into one of the plants, as a sacrifice to form a connection between us and the spiritual realm, to summon the awakening of our Ancestors.

Through further study of the concept of Ancestor veneration, I learned that they should be considered a part of our family. Since they've crossed over, some of them have been divinely entrusted with our spiritual development. They have been directed to watch over us and guide us, but since many of us have been brainwashed, we consider the spirit world to be evil. The altar is a way to communicate with them, and some believe, they are the most under-utilized population because we are too afraid or don't know we can engage them.

I was confident that Granddaddy, Grandmommy, Auntie, and Uncle George meant me no harm from the other side and created an altar in my living room in their memory. I knew that they loved me and could help guide me in the right direction if only I asked. I knew I missed them and had had a few dreams about them. I found the perfect place in my home and placed their photos, a plant, Grandmommy's wedding ring, a glass of water, and a piece of fruit on the altar, as a way to present an offering. Two-way communication works in the spirit realm as well, so the water and fruit were my way of giving while asking to receive. Sometimes I put Granddaddy's favorite candy, peanut brittle on the altar as an offering.

The Fertile Ground song, "Spirit World" resonated with me as I became more comfortable and open to the idea of communicating with my loved ones.

"I want to know the role of my soul in the spirit world..."

"I want to know the role of my soul in the spirit world..."

Goyzam, The Beloved One

In June of 2015, Ambassador Feo invited me to an event sponsored by The Cameroon Royal Council. The Cameroon Royal Council is an apolitical organization with a vision to promote Cameroon's culture in the diaspora (def: people settled far from their ancestral homelands[28]), among other initiatives. It was being held at Howard University in Washington, D.C., and was set to begin at 6 p.m. I'd intentionally arrived early at 5:30 p.m., to assist with set-up. Funny enough, this became one of my first lessons on 'colored people's time' 'aka' 'CP Time,'. When I walked into the venue at 5:30 p.m. it was empty - not a single soul was in sight. It took another two hours for everyone to arrive and another hour for the Ambassador and his family to make their grand entrance. I learned then that African and Western cultures relate to time in distinctly different ways.

It was a festive occasion and the room filled up quickly, as each family brought a dish to share. I sat in the front row along with my guest, Janaye. The drummers came out first, then the children and teen dancers joined in, with great energy. This was the customary protocol to welcome the Ambassador and his family into the gathering. All of the attendees rose to their feet. They clapped as the Ambassador, his wife, and their children took their seats at the front of the room. The performers, dressed in traditional Cameroonian attire, which included colorful embroidery in black, red, yellow, orange, and greens, danced directly in front of the family. A lot was going on at one time, and I was taking it all in. I felt privileged to have been invited to witness something so fascinating.

After the dancers and drummers ended, Ambassador Feo came to the front of the room for announcements. Surprisingly he began to share some of the details of our meeting and interactions with the audience. He told them that I'd traced my DNA to the Mafa people living in the Extreme North, and everyone clapped. I was a little embarrassed because I wasn't aware that he'd planned to make me a part of the program. He invited me to join him at the podium and presented me with an official certificate with my new Cameroonian name, Goyzam, which meant *Beloved One*. They were using this special occasion to welcome me 'home.'

Out of nowhere, three ladies whisked me away into the restroom and began dressing me in a green and yellow dress. They wrapped my hair and told me that I would be presented to the community. Before I could catch my breath and ask if there was anything specific that I needed to do, they hurriedly walked me back into the auditorium to stand before the Ambassador and his family. The drummers started playing again, and there was little ole' me, in a standing-room-only auditorium filled with my people, my countrymen of Cameroon.

A few words were spoken from the women who'd dressed me and whatever she said caused the crowd to clap. Things were quickly moving. So, I tried my best to be present. Instinctively, I turned and bowed in gratitude towards the Ambassador and his family. I was officially considered a CamAmerican, a Cameroonian American, and I was overwhelmed with gratitude. The experience of reconnecting with my fellow CamAmericans, to being given a beautiful, traditional Mafa name from the land of my maternal lineage, was exponentially more than I'd ever dreamed of. I couldn't wait to share the news with everyone I knew!

The Birth of FromJerZtoMe.com

Later that summer, during Essence Fest, in New Orleans, I attended the Walker's Legacy Awards Brunch. Walker's Legacy is a national woman in business collective whose mission is to increase the number of women entrepreneurs of color by improving access to key resources. The brunch was for woman entrepreneurs (of which I was not one) as the guest of my friend, Janaye, who was being honored. On the real, I was picking at my food and looking around the room. I was not absorbing too much of what was said. In my head I was like…I've got a "J-O-B", I was getting a decent paycheck and benefits…why on earth would I want to "struggle" in the world of the entrepreneur? The take-away of the event was that each woman should consider entrepreneurship *and* should have purchased at least one URL (Uniform Resource Locator), which in layman's terms is a web address, by the next brunch in the summer of 2016.

As I sat there, eating my dessert, I began to think that though I wasn't interested in entrepreneurship at the very least, I could consider purchasing a URL. I was always told that I told great stories, so maybe I could share some of my unsolicited musings on a blog platform. As the brunch ended, I walked out into the sweltering NOLA heat, heading back to peruse the vendors in the Convention Center, when the words *"From New Jersey to Me"*, mysteriously popped into my head. It did have a ring but sounded too long. I was trying to visualize what it would look like written or the ease of typing it. FromNewJerseyToMe.com? Nah, I didn't like that. I kept walking then the little voice said "FromJerseytoMe.com".

A lightbulb went off in my head, and I stepped inside of a hotel lobby to cool off a bit and to write it out the URL in the note section of my iPhone. I wanted to *see* what it looked like written out. It still didn't look right, so I truncated Jersey and wrote it out as JerZ. Then I re-typed it in my browser so I could get the visual and right there on the spot, FromJerZToMe.com was born. It was short and easy to type. I immediately called, Chers to run it by her. I told her the different variations, and she agreed, it sounded like a cool name for a blog, so I immediately got on GoDaddy.com and purchased my URL for $9.99 for the year. Voila! I was an official "Blogger"! Me?! A "Blogger"?! I still wasn't too sure about that because though I loved reading blogs, I never thought about writing one.

Then the fear set in…
What if "they" don't like what I have to say?

What if I reveal too much?

What if I lose some friends over my opinion on current events?
That's when I asked myself, "Who in the hell is "they"?"

"Why do "they" always have something to say?"

"Why do we give the "theys" so much credit?

I reasoned it came with the territory, that this would help me exercise my 'not-giving-a-crap-what-people-say" muscle and started writing immediately. I had so many amazing things going on in my life, and this was a great way to share them on a larger platform. Writing each blog was like birthing a new baby, sort of like writing this book. My first blog post was a photo of the continent of Africa. I enjoyed sharing all of my thoughts leading up to my trip to Cameroon. I blogged about packing, the vaccinations, my African Ancestry results, my hopes for the trip.

I was glad I got out of my own way that day, FromJerZtoMe.com became therapeutic for me during some personal and world-wide crazy times! Sometimes I'd get so inspired on a topic that the blog post wrote itself, like the one about my naming ceremony at Howard University, just the month before. I shared my entire experience, posting the photos, and the certificate on my shiny, new blog. Other times it took a few weeks for me to finalize, but once I had agonized over the finished product enough, I would nervously hit publish! In the beginning, I focused on the number of likes and comments but quickly learned that wasn't important. The people who are supposed to read it did…and offered so much positive feedback, and for that I was grateful.

Sannu, Cameroon!
(Translation: Hello, Cameroon! In the Fulfulde language.)

October 2015 couldn't come soon enough, I was ready to set foot on Mother Africa and, more specifically, in Cameroon. I felt like I'd waited a lifetime to experience this reconnection to my roots. I'd had plenty of opportunities to visit Africa in the past but never Cameroon so, I promised myself that I wouldn't step foot on the Continent unless it was there first. My dream was coming true! After a few months of preparation, including a few painful vaccinations, Janaye and I jetted off to Cameroon, with a contingent of travelers, mostly entrepreneurs and politicos, to connect with our gracious host, Raoul.

At exactly 4:46 p.m. on October 9, 2015, I stepped foot on African soil in Douala, the largest city in and the capital of Cameroon. That blast of heat and funk that hit my face when I disembarked from the plane reminded me that after eight years of yearning, I was finally in the homeland of my foremothers. There was a stirring sensation in my stomach as we walked through the airport. I was using my senses to absorb it all. I noted pungent smells, amplified sounds, and stimulating energy.

Raoul enlisted security to take us from the airport to the hotel. After a bit of confusion, we finally settled in, and while lying in my bed that night, I kept repeating to myself, "You are in Africa!" "No, really, Tisha, Wendi, Kora, and Goyzam…you are finally in Africa!" I even took a photo of my foot touching the ground for the first time and posted it on FromJerZtoMe.com.

Our main purpose of this trip was to participate in Raoul's African-America Business Summit, a trade mission to learn about investment opportunities in Cameroon's expanding sectors, including health, energy, and infrastructure. As a guest on one of the panels, I shared my feelings about having traced my roots to Cameroon, and after my speech, the entire audience shouted, "Welcome home, Wendi!", in unison, then broke out in song. All I could do was smile and turn a shade of pink because they were so happy for me to be returning.

The week was a whirlwind of meetings, tours, trains, taxis, traffic, new smells, sights, and foods. Our delegation had the great privilege of being interviewed on radio station *Ell'FM 104.2* where I got to share my thoughts on reconnecting to the continent. After we handled our business each day, we embarked on a tour or visited the street markets. I bought unique and traditional Cameroonian art and jewelry to bring back to my family and friends. I blogged every moment of it, complete with photos and videos of this incredible adventure.

One of the most immediate and mind-blowing observations I made was how euro-centric Cameroon seemed to me; I'd never expected to see the citizens in the city dressed in such formal corporate attire. When we ventured into the smaller villages, I saw more of what I would consider traditional African garments with prints, skirts, and headwraps. It was funny to see the similarities of the women's hairstyles with their colorful braids, weaves, and wigs, which would have fit in perfectly with women living in D.C., Baltimore, Atlanta, or Detroit. The Western influence was stronger in Cameroon than I'd anticipated.

We attempted to visit Bimbia, an old slave-trading port situated more than an hour away from the economic capital of Douala. Some of the locals told me that it was considered "The Door of No Return," just like the dungeons on Goree Island in Dakar, Senegal. I later learned that by 1472, the Portuguese had arrived, and Bimbia suddenly grew to become a significant slave route through which many Cameroonians, between the 1500s - 1700s, passed through to reach plantations abroad.[29] We made our way to the historical site. Though the torrential rains were easing up, we still found the terrain was too muddy and rocky for our small car to make the trek. I was disappointed because I felt compelled to visit the site to pay homage to my ancestral grandmother. Had she been forced to make the 821-mile trip, from the Extreme North heading south along the coast only to arrive at Bimbia to be stolen from her land? How on earth did I make it to Cameroon only to be blocked by the mud and rocks? I believe that timing is everything, and for some reason, it just wasn't my time. Though I haven't made it there yet, the spirit of Bimbia is calling me, and I vow to return one day.

After we left, Bimbia, we visited Seme Beach in the town of Limbe, located in the Southwest Province of Cameroon. Due to the past lava flows of Mount Cameroon, the sand was black, red and silky, something I'd never seen before. Being forced to leave the shores of her Cameroonian home forever, I reflected on what my ancestral grandmother's experience may have been, as I sat near the ocean on that cloudy, humid, windy day. The water and foam were gliding along the sand within inches of my shoes. So, I took them off and stayed along the very edge of the rough waters. I did this just enough to let the warmth of the Atlantic Ocean caress my bare feet. Finally, I was able to dig them deeper into the soil…something I'd dreamed.

While the rest of the group was enjoying the beach, I took some time alone to get still. While looking out into the water, I reflected on how terrified my ancestral grandmother must have been. Was she ever warned about impending danger, or even aware of what was happening to her? Did she cry out loud guttural sobs or suppress her terror within her throat, womb, and heart? Was she a little girl yearning for her mom and dad or a newlywed wondering why her beloved's strong arms weren't coming to rescue her? Was she a teacher, artisan, homemaker, or healer? Was she the life of the party, a good dancer, or have a flair for fashion? I longed to know more about who she was as a human being.

As is customary, I wanted to make an offering to express my gratitude for her sacrifice and honor her pain. Unfortunately, I was traveling light, so I hadn't thought to bring anything of significance with me. However, I dug around in my travel bag only to find a piece of sugared ginger, that I'd brought over as a snack from Trader Joe's. For me, the ginger represented the bittersweet occasion. Then I fished out a single penny from the bottom of my bag. I designated it to represent the 'change' in me because of this trip and the experiences it provided me.

In a whispered voice, over the crashing waves, I introduced myself to her and said a little prayer of gratitude. I told her about my journey to make it back to 'our' homeland and that I'd hoped she was proud of the woman I was becoming. I told her that I was grateful for her sacrifice and sorry for all of the pain, anxiety, uncertainty, and torture she experienced. If she had not survived and if her daughters for generations after her had not survived the trauma, I literally would not exist. With that, I threw the penny and ginger as far into the ocean as I could. Usually a big ole' cry baby, I'd imagined this moment differently…I assumed I would have been overly emotional and weepy but instead, I felt uncharacteristically calm, peaceful, and full of gratitude.

Afterward, I rejoined the rest of my group for photos, and right before we started wiping the sand off of our feet and putting our shoes back on, it struck me to engrave my names in the sand. With a piece of rock, I wrote Tisha, Wendi, Kora, and Goyzam was here and added the Ankh representing everlasting life. I also filled a small bag of that black, silky sand to take home to place on my Ancestral alter. Now, I felt connected enough to my maternal, ancestral grandmother also to ask her guidance on issues that were important to me. This served as my symbol that I still live on through my ancestral grandmother...as does my daughter, Sydni, and her future daughters for generations to come. Our X-chromosome is inextricably connected to our grandmother from the Mafa people of the Extreme North of Cameroon on the Continent of Africa.

Unfortunately, I never got to visit Mokolo, the actual geographic area in the Extreme North, where many of the Mafa people still reside. Besides the fact that the trip is an 8-hour flight from Douala, the infamous Boko Harem had recently just kidnapped a group of girls near the border so, the US State Department released a travel warning for anyone traveling in the region.[30]

Even though it took eight-years from the day I got my DNA test results until I set foot on African soil, I was still so gratified that I'd manifested my vision of visiting Cameroon. I never knew how or when it would happen but just had the faith that it would be so. I remain so grateful for Janaye and Raoul, for allowing me to join them on such a memorable adventure. Moving forward, I noticed that I held my head up a bit higher, felt more connected to an actual country and people, as I'd finally been able to add another piece to the puzzle of my identity.

Upon my return from Cameroon, I felt a bit overwhelmed as I needed to absorb and understand what I'd just experienced. I'd gotten some of the answers I was looking for, yet an entirely new crop of questions arose. Since Africa was so rich in intellectual, natural and human resources, why had it become a victim of colonization, brainwashing, and corruption? In the past, Americans were warned not to visit Africa, that it was "the Dark Continent" and not civilized or safe. In Cameroon, I realized the importance for Africans all over the diaspora to cut out the "middle man" (euro-centric influences and opinions), and connect with our brothers and sisters on the continent to create solutions on how we can support each other.

I'd visited Cameroon and paid my respects to the maternal side of my family and was now itching to explore the paternal side. Since we already knew our ancestral paternal grandmother was from the Temne people living in Sierra Leone, once again my biological father took African Ancestry's PatriClan test. I didn't even have a good guess, but during our Thanksgiving dinner, Gina Paige, the Co-Founder and President, of African Ancestry, delivered our results via video. I'd encouraged everyone to place their guess in a hat to see if anyone would guess correctly.

Everyone was intently listening as Gina announced that our ancestral paternal grandfather was from Germany. Two of my sisters and one cousin guessed Germany correctly! "Yeah! Germany...don't be alarmed!" Gina's voice advised from the video. "Well, too late, Gina!" I thought. To say I was a bit blown would be an understatement. Not sure why, though, I knew there was a 35 percent chance I would have someone of European descent in my family.

Per the African Ancestry Web site, it notes that sixty-five percent (65%) of the paternal lineages that they trace result in African ancestry.[31] There is a 35 percent chance that the results will not be African – the fact is, white men were having black babies. After more research, I discovered that Germany was among the European countries to participate in *The Scramble for Africa* [32] between 1881 and 1914. This was potentially a case of a German human trafficker (read: enslaved person owner) raping my African grandmother beginning this family line.

When I heard Germany, the first thing that popped into my brain was Hitler, Oktoberfest, and beer...all of which I had no clue. I am still processing it and searching for more information to help me put this into a better context. The bottom line is that I am grateful to be able to add another leaf to a branch on my family tree.

The Journey to Kemet

The travel bug bit me, and I was inspired by my first adventure to visit more African countries. Sierra Leone was still on the bucket list. However, I got the opportunity to join Anthony (Tony) Browder, Cultural Historian and Author of *"Nile Valley Contributions to Civilization"*[33] on a field trip to Kemet (Egypt). (Kemet is the original name meaning "land of the blacks"[34]). I'd originally told myself that I could not afford, nor did I deserve an experience in Kemet, especially since I had just returned from Cameroon. I talked myself out of a potentially amazing opportunity until I started doing some deep self-reflection while 'sitting on Thema's pot' that I recognized that I was repeating my old cycle of getting stuck in limiting thought patterns and beliefs. She reminded me that I deserved everything good. Why not Kemet? Nobody was holding me back from this trip but me. I had the time, resources, and desire to visit East Africa to explore the Nile Valley Civilization, the first historical record of civilization in the world, and the origins of human evolution.

Finally, I got out of my way and green-lit my Kemet trip. It could not have come at a better time because the world was going crazy, right before our very eyes. On July 5, 2016, Alton Sterling was shot six times at close range while selling CDs at a local convenience store in Baton Rouge, Louisiana.[35] The very next day, Philando Castile, a 32-year-old black man, was murdered by Officer Jeronimo Yanez, while his fiancé filmed part of the incident, in Minnesota.[36] These senseless acts were becoming too overwhelming. I could feel the pressure and anxiety rising within me. The media replayed these incidences ad nauseum and I needed an emotional reprieve from this heavy feeling of loss and anger. Most people were unaware that continually watching those murders causes emotional trauma and anxiety in the human body. I certainly felt the effects of it. According to The Counted, a project launched by The Guardian that tracks police killings in America, Sterling was the 558th person police killed in America in 2016.[37] Even more startling was the fact we were only halfway through the year.

I woke up that morning, excited to finally head to John F. Kennedy airport in Queens, New York, only to hear of yet *another* shooting in Dallas, Texas. What had started as a peaceful protest against the killings of Sterling and Castile quickly turned violent as a black, lone gunman, Micah Johnson, *allegedly* killed five police officers.[38] The Dallas incident was on everyone's mind while we waited for our flight. The TVs in the airport were still playing and re-playing each account. I felt both guilt and peace at the same time. I was grateful to be leaving the country during such an emotionally volatile time because hell...I needed a break. All of us in the melanated community were clear that this, police violence, murder, and terror against our community was not new. This current iteration just happened to be on display for the world to see via camera phones, Facebook Lives, and CNN, but it still didn't feel like change was coming anytime soon.

We finally arrived in Cairo and made our way to the hotel. From the pool, I was amazed to see the Great Pyramid (Mir is the name the ancients called the pyramids) standing so majestically in the distance. I had to pinch myself to take it all in. Wow! I'd done it; I was here in Kemet, my second trip to Africa in less than eight months! We took off at break-neck pace over the next 14 days. We visited some of the most amazing wonders of the world, from The Pyramids at Giza to marvel at the pyramids of Khufu, Kafara, and Menkara (these are the three that you always see in photos) and Heremakhet (incorrectly called 'the Sphinx').

Our guide, Tony Browder, imparted on us that we were embarking on a field trip, *not* a vacation, and to consider ourselves *'spiritual sojourners'* versus tourists. That like a butterfly breaking free from its cocoon, we too would have our transformation. He called it a *'Kemetamorphosis'*. He promised that after this experience, we would return home different people. Over the 14-days, we toured the pyramids, tombs, and museums during the day and participated in lectures every evening. Our on-site tour guide, Ahmed Hashem, fondly called us his "Faaamiiily" from our first meeting. Every day after that, when you heard those words, you knew it was time to motivate to the next stop. We called ourselves that for the remainder of the trip.

These Mir (Pyramids) were massive, and to this day, no one knows how they were built. Due to my severe claustrophobia, I lingered along the outside, while the rest of the group toured inside. That heat was unlike heat I'd felt before, dry and hard. I wore light-colored, loose-fitting clothing, and wrapped my head with a scarf. The sun was so intense, I could feel it searing my scalp through each part in my locs. We visited some of the most awe-inspiring sites inclusive of the following: Necropolis of Thebes on the West Bank, the Valley of the Kings, the Temple of Queen Hatshepsut, and the Egyptian Museum. We swam in the Nile River, as well as visited a Nubian village where we donated school supplies and received an invitation to the home of a local family where a woman let us hold her pet alligator and gave us henna tattoos.

Over dinner one night, our tour guide, Ahmed Hashem, asked me what my role in the US revolution was. He knew a little something about revolutions after having risked family, life, and limb to participate in the two most recent revolutions in Kemet.[39] The US was on center-stage as countries around the world were watching the turmoil happening on our soil. The news was non-stop, portraying the stories of the murders of melanated people in the streets and the aftermath of mothers, wives, and children in tears at press conferences. "Where was the outrage?" he questioned. "Why weren't black people taking action, forcing the government to understand their plight?" Ahmed asked some great questions.

Unfortunately, I didn't have any real answers. I felt embarrassed, sad, confused, and honestly unprepared to offer any substantive answer. Of course, I had participated in what I call 'the modern cycle of grief' by marching in one-day protests or posting the name of the newest victim on social media in hashtag form, but that was the extent of it. Back home, it felt like the perfect storm was brewing. Presidential hopeful, Donald Trump, was ramping up his campaign of hate. During the Republican Convention, he was seemingly giving the green light for white cops to continue to shoot melanated bodies at will, with no recourse. I became more interested in what the nuts and bolts of a true revolution required. Portrayed to be sexy in the reflection of them, was one depiction of the revolutions of the past. But I am sure those who'd shed blood, would offer a different perspective.

The Merriam Webster dictionary[40] defines revolution in the following ways:

Def. Rev·o·lu·tion, (noun) a forcible overthrow of a government or social order in favor of a new system.
2a: a sudden, radical, or complete change
b: a fundamental change in political organization
c: activity or movement designed to effect fundamental changes in the socioeconomic situation
d: a fundamental change in the way of thinking about or visualizing something: a change of paradigm

Synonyms include: transformation, shift, innovation, upheaval

In my opinion, since folks couldn't even give up watching football to support Colin Kaepernick's protest,[41] which was to highlight police brutality. Considering a full-fledged revolution, to be undertaken by the American people, seemed unlikely. According to the definition above, I'm not sure that our community was interested enough or in the words of my Soror, Fannie Lou Hamer, sick and tired of being sick and tired [42] enough to deploy a long-term strategy and coordinated effort. If we were to contemplate mounting a tactic like this, once it began, there could be no retreat, no fear, complete solidarity, and unity among *all* people who care about life, love, and liberty. With that said, I still believe that marching and protests work up to a point, but when they prove to be ineffective, then there must be a more effective way of making our voices heard.

That all seemed like a tall order. Sitting with Ahmed that day, hearing him talk about the lengths that he and his fellow citizens went through to demand change, inspired me to think more deeply.

What exactly was my role? Who would listen to me anyway? I'd always felt anger about the treatment of melanated people but just wasn't sure how to harness it in a productive and impactful way.

The part of the definition stated that *"a fundamental change in the way of thinking about or visualizing something: a change of paradigm"* resonated with me the most. I began reflecting on many of the situations I'd attracted to myself, both good and bad, and my role in them. If I was honest with myself, 50 percent of the crap that I'd experienced was due to my negative thinking and actions. While floating down the Nile River one, beautiful African evening, I became still and present, noticing how full and striking the moon looked. I took a deep inhale of the Nubian air, listened to the water crash against the tender, and the excited chatter of my *Kemetamorphosis Family* journeying with me. I felt the mist of the water splash on my face and the salty taste of my tears mixed with the Nile River water on my lips. I felt peaceful, hopeful, prayerful, and protected. Most of all, I felt grateful to myself for having been brave enough to know that I was finally getting it…I needed to think and be different to attract different results. It was clicking that I was the co-creator of my life, along with The Creator, and once given a vision; it was my job to take it to the next level. Floating down the Nile River that day just made it clearer that I was on the right path and upon my return, there were some things that I was going to have to change.

There was some residual disappointment that I'd made it to Cameroon without being able to visit Bimbia. I didn't want to go out like a sucker and miss my opportunity to descend on a shaky, 30-feet ladder to visit the 2,700-year-old burial tomb of Karakhamun[43], the First Ak Priest of Amun at Karnak Temple (circa 747 and 525 BC). Or did I? I'd been severely claustrophobic most of my life, hating to have the covers pulled over my head or to be underwater too long. You would never find me intentionally venturing into small crawl spaces.

The most memorable time that the feeling of claustrophobia attacked my nervous system was in 1985 at the Eatontown Roller Rink standing in line for the UTFO and LL Cool J concert. The crowd was pushing and yelling in an attempt to bum-rush the door. Swaying back and forth, with lifted feet off the ground, I was petrified. For many years after that, in crowds or tight spaces, I experienced the same quickening of the heart, fast breath, my fight or flight response would kick in, my palms would get sweaty, and my eyes would dart around looking for the nearest escape route.

So, you see, it took a lot-more convincing, but alas, I was in Kemet so, I put on my big girl panties and began descending into the tomb. With the support of my Kemetamorphosis Family cheering me on, I made my way down from top to bottom of the ladder. I took my time, white-knuckling each narrow rung, ensuring my booted foot was planted firmly on every-single-step. I could hear my friend M'Bwebe encouraging me from the top, "…that's it!" "…you got it!" "…almost there!" In my head, I was saying, "Lord, please don't let me plunge 30-feet to my death, out here in these Kemetic streets, in this here tomb!"

The scene at the bottom took my breath away. I was one of a few select people blessed enough to ever enter such a sacred space. A place that had been disrespected by tomb robbers but still housed a special spirit. Yes! I'd done it! This action was one of the first steps of me doing something different and new and not allowing my fears to stop me.

A few days later, in Luxor, we went to a spice and oil shop owned by a well-respected healer and herbalist. He asked for a volunteer to come to the front of the room for a special demonstration. I had no idea what that, but in the spirit of being open and trying new things, I raised my hand and was selected. Timidly, I sat in his chair in front of the entire Family. I felt comfortable enough, so I closed my eyes and mentally prepared for the unknown. He used his hands to scan my body. He started from the top of my head down my back to my abdomen. Feeling my mild anxiety, he whispered to me to allow whatever emotion that I felt surface freely, regardless if it was a laugh or a cry. At first, I was cool, thinking in my head, I am not going to embarrass myself in front of these folks. I've got this. Unexpectedly though, I started to feel some emotions bubbling up inside of me. I wasn't clear on the root, so I continued to sit back while he scanned my body.

The entire scan took about five minutes; after completion, he explained that he could sense that I had poor digestion, which Dr. Mines had diagnosed me with a few years back. With that, he invited me to his private office because he had perceived some other more personal information that he didn't want to share with the group. I was nervous now. Was he going to tell me something bad? I followed him into his small office, which looked much like a doctor's office, complete with a medical table and instruments, and waited patiently until he returned and closed the door. Though there was a language barrier, he stepped directly in my face, and we stood nose-to-nose for a few seconds. He gently took both of my hands in his and told me that he could detect that I was looking for love and was sad. He told me not to begin another relationship with anyone who didn't truly love me and, most importantly for me to be sure I loved myself.

I wondered, "Who was this guy and how in the heck does he know all of that?" I wasn't even sure that I'd acknowledged those emotions to myself. With that, the tears started welling up in my eyes. I tried with all of my might to suppress this energy rising through my throat that I just knew would manifest as an ugly cry. I immediately sucked it back down and noticing what I'd just done, he squeezed my hands again and said, "It's okay, my sister, let it out." With that, I wailed. He quickly ran across the room to get me some tissues. I was so embarrassed but had no control over the tears streaming down my cheeks like a waterfall. He continued, noting that he could sense fear in my spirit. I told him that I was considering making some major life changes very soon, and they seemed a bit daunting. He encouraged me to approach things very slowly and carefully, and that ultimately, everything would work out fine. He gave me some oils for sensuality and my Sacral Chakra and a blended tea for my digestion.

I was astounded! How in the heck could he read me so well after only scanning my body for five minutes? It was uncomfortable, but this medicine man had just confirmed what I'd probably known, deep within, and If I was going to honor myself, it was time for something new. Between visiting the historic sites and Tony's lectures each evening, I'd most certainly had a personal *Kemetamorphosis* during my two-week field experience in Kemet.

Below are a few of the most impactful takeaways and confirmations that Tony imparted to or group of spiritual sojourners:

*I tweaked a few of them while taking notes to make sense to me.

1. Attract master teachers and listen (my favorite one)
2. Understand that my thoughts proceed my speech, so be mindful of them
3. Always act with discretion
4. Have confidence in my abilities
5. Give myself freedom from resentment
6. Believe in myself
7. Go out into the world to fulfill my destiny

I'd gotten my marching orders and felt educated, empowered, and enlightened to move to the next level of my spiritual and emotional evolution. I felt like the Ancestors were telling me they'd been waiting for me **to choose** to awaken and heal. I wasn't sure how it would all play out, but I knew that I was committed to embarking on the journey. I purchased a beautiful gold Ankh in Kemet, representing everlasting life, and added that to my Ancestral alter. One day, I too would become an Ancestor, the decisions I made, and the actions I took, could potentially affect the next seven generations after me. So, I wanted to begin to take steps to make sure I was worthy of the honor of Sydni's children and great-great-grandchildren. Like the song "Remember Me" from Pixar's Oscar-winning movie, *Coco,* I hope they will remember me enough to place a photo of me on their alter and speak my name with pride.

Kendrick Lamar's song, "Momma", from his album, *To Pimp a Butterfly,* was on constant rotation during that entire trip. It resonated with my spirit so intensely, not just for the laid-back, funky-assed beat but for the lyrics and Lalah Hathaway's haunting melodious voice singing…

"We've been waiting for you…"

"Waiting for you, waiting for you…"

"Waiting for youuu…"

Synchronicity?

Less than three weeks after visiting Kemet, I was in Havana, Cuba, to study yoga, the dances of the Orisha[44]. Additionally, I was there to visit the Orisha museum in Regla in Colonial Habana and to learn more about Castro's revolt in January of 1959. How synchronistic was that? I'd just begun studying revolutions, and Cuba was one of the most well-known countries for its revolution. As a result of my Kemetamorphosis experience, I had a fire in my belly. I was preparing myself for the most earth-shattering experience ever, an internal revolution of self-reflection, and ultimately self-love. Since I couldn't speak for or control anyone else, I knew this work started in the mirror. I decided to become intentional about the energy I exuded. I had to become more deliberate about bringing clarity, peace, and love, to any given situation. As Vikki said, my only two choices were love or fear. I was choosing love – radical self-love. It was time to begin changing my thoughts and beliefs for a new system. Though I wasn't crystal clear on the best way to approach it, I knew that with the tools of my guides enough prayer, meditation, and stillness, the ancestors would reveal it to me.

Sound Scape: "Momma" by Kendrick Lamar

Kemet (July, 2016)

Seme Beach, Limbe Province, Cameroon
Photo: Raoul Keddy (October 15, 2015)

My Discoveries & Reflections

Mommy got me a scrapbook with the title Wondering Wendi as an ode to my love for travel. I was encouraged to explore at an early age and went full-force. I enjoyed eating new foods, seeing unique cultures and lands. My travel gave me a unique perspective on life and pushed me out of my comfort zone.

Your Reflections
CHAPTER 7

THE CHALLENGE:

By this time next year, I challenge you to have done something totally exciting, new, and out of your comfort zone. Get an accountability partner or don't share it with a soul.

Will you write your memoir, quit your job, allow yourself to fall in love, travel, or hit the gym?

Take a few minutes to get still and think about it.

List two of your initial ideas below.

_____
_____
_____
_____
_____

Date: _____

wendicherry.com   @AwakenAndHeal

List one action step you can take by the end of the month for each below.

_____
_____
_____
_____
_____

Date: _____

Revisit your ideas in one year to check in on your success.
Good luck!

Have you ever considered taking the African Ancestry test?

Why or why not?

_____
_____
_____
_____

Visit africanancestry.com to learn more.

Write down your feelings about honoring your ancestors.
Is this a ritual you would be open to considering?
Why or why not?

_____
_____
_____
_____

wendicherry.com   @AwakenAndHeal

169

Have you ever considered making an alter to your ancestors?

If yes, list the names of the people you would like to honor in that way.

Note: Only consider the ones who made you feel loved.

_____
_____
_____
_____
_____

Chapter 8: The Butterfly Is I

"Shine already, it's time already!" – Beyoncé

2016: The Ending of a Cycle

I'd had so many 'aha moments' in 2015 and was hungry to explore more. Right after my adventures in Cameroon, Kemet, and Cuba, I was on a mission to find *MY* why, *MY* purpose, *MY* calling, *MY* destiny. I was searching for the reason The Creator decided that I needed to enter this realm at this exact time in history. I lost interest in things that had once held my attention and taken up so much of my time. I began praying more but not in the traditional Christian way; I began to meditate in the morning and those times I 'stayed woke,' versus falling asleep, I had real breakthroughs. I started not giving two shits about what other people thought. Then I began attracting new people with infectious energy who shared new (to me) revelations for me to consider. They liked similar music, clothing, food, and made me feel safe in their presence.

Right after my 45th birthday, in 2015, I read an article titled *"2016 Numerology Predictions - Personal Year"* [45] in anticipation of what I could expect for the upcoming year. I intended to enter 2016 with a fresh approach and look at everything through a new lens and, most importantly, to be more open and flexible. Remember, historically, being open and flexible were not my jam. Not to mention neither was numerology because I'd been told it was 'of the devil,' but here I was exploring new concepts. Yay, me! I had to calculate a few formulas first, for me to understand what the numbers meant. For some reason, I felt led to modify the formula a bit, by not including the birth year, and was startled at what came up.

Step One: The formula was to calculate the **Universal Year Number** by adding the numbers from the year and reducing them down to a single digit.

Since the year was **2016**, the calculation was:

2 + 0 + 1 + 6 = 9

Step Two: I only added my month and day, **October 26,** excluding the year, and the calculation was.

1 + 0 + 2 + 6 = 9

Both nines! According to the numerologists who wrote this article, **2016** was considered a **number nine (9) year**, which signified the end of a cycle. I had just turned 45 years old at the time and started freaking out a little bit when I calculated **4+5 = 9**, which, *again*, means the end of the cycle. So, between the Universal Year Number, my birth month, and date and my current age, everything was popping up nines!

The article also stated among other things that the year 2016, was time for:

Completion + Rest + Forgiveness

As I researched the number nine, I found an expansive list of attributes, on Numerologist, Joanne Walmsley's Web site,[46] which was very reassuring. This was all very fascinating because, for years, every time I looked up, I'd see the number sequence of *1-0-2-6.* Whether on street signs, a clock, TV, even the time someone texted or sent me an email. Once I tuned in, I realized it was a regular occurrence, so I looked it up and found it's a very real phenomenon called synchronicity[47] (meaningful coincidences). It goes above mere chance and statistical probability; because numbers, counting, and math are universal amongst all cultures.

Again, according to Joanne's site, here where the attributes of each of the numbers *1-0-2-6* were:

Number 1: Promotes positivity and optimism, creation and new beginnings, self-leadership, assertiveness, inspiration, achievement, and success. (Definitely many of the characteristics I was working on.)

Number 0: Carries the vibration of the 'God force' and Universal Energies, and emphasizes developing my spiritual aspects and represents the beginning of my spiritual journey. (Becoming intentional about listening to my intuition and higher-self to find my answers.)

Number 2: Vibrations of adaptability, duality, service, and duty, balance, and harmony, faith and trust in *MY* divine life purpose and soul mission. (All lessons I was experiencing.)

Number 6: Relates to service, home, family, love, nurturing, responsibility, reliability, honesty, and integrity. (These are all non-negotiables in my opinion.)

Come on now! This didn't sound like the devil to me. If anything, it felt like a wink from The Creator, confirming that I was on the right path. It felt very peaceful and comforting so, every time I see **1-0-2-6**, I take the entire minute to sing, *"Ten-Twenty-Siiiii-*

hhhiiix", take a few deep breaths, twerk, and remind myself of how blessed I am to be alive at this exact moment.

Diving even deeper, the article proclaimed that something in my life would come to an end **BUT** I didn't have to consider it a bad thing and to remember that endings could also be considered blessings. It also noted there would be a great amount of loss. That part was true, remember all of the celebs that transitioned that year?! Muhammed Ali, Natalie Cole, Maurice White, Phife, Prince, and David Bowie. Dang!

I was still tripping because since my birthday is October 26th and the upcoming year was going to be 2016, that meant that my birthday would fall on **10/26/2016** that year! I had to take a breath (…you should too!). Now, remember, I would have never, ever, ever considered entertaining such a notion, but the way this article laid it out so plainly, it resonated deeply within me. I could feel, with every fiber of my being, that I was on the cusp of something huge. I couldn't put my finger on it just yet, but my intuition (which I was just beginning to get in tune with) told me so, and *finally*, I believed her! This was certainly an interesting perspective that I could choose to consider moving forward – really, what could it hurt? I was both intrigued and inspired by the potential of things to come. My main fear was the loss part, was I going to transition or worse yet, someone in my family? I chose to worry less about the what-ifs and decided to dream about the infinite possibilities that were in store for me. Then, I began unpacking the main themes for 2016, which were *completion, rest*, and *forgiveness*.

Completion

There were a few situations, people, and things that I needed to close the loop on. I was good at beginning a thing, but my follow-up could be a bit suspect at times. I decided to take the advice of the article and incorporate the following into my life:

- Learn to meditate and practice deep breathing.

- Declutter! Throw away old papers or clothes I hadn't worn. This action aligned perfectly with what was going on in my life. I was in the process of buying a condo and had a lot of decluttering and packing to do.

- Finally, I needed to finish all of those lingering projects I'd started but had been putting off.

- There were also a few relationships that I needed to end, which though scary to contemplate, were necessary for my growth.

Rest

Around this same time, I'd been introduced to the concept of BEING more versus DOING more. This was another way to incorporate rest into my life. Whoa! Can you say mind-blowing?! It almost went against everything our society teaches us about hustling, grinding, not sleeping, making it happen, no pain - no gain. Some people even bragged about how hard they worked, like that made them better than the next person. Historically, melanated women conditioned themselves to think they were Super Woman, and to put on their cape every morning to go out and fight the world. To be everything to everyone, many times neglecting themselves.

The consideration was to practice *just* BEING, which felt so foreign. You mean, don't try to regulate every single, solitary detail of a particular thing? Come on, really? I didn't even know the look, taste, or smell of that. I had no frame of reference for not white-knuckling every outcome. I have worked in event production for the past 25-years. The production schedule was my bible. I needed to know the who, what, where, when, and why to do my job at a high level. My family began calling me "Clipboard Cherry" because I always added an extra layer of details around every event, big or small. Annoying, I know. It seemed to be the only way I could feel comfortable that it would go the right way. Ha!

I also thought about the old joke that some island people had such an aggressive work ethic that they worked five jobs. Well, as I pondered that concept more, I questioned how healthy and happy could one authentically be if they were hustling and grinding their life away on these five jobs?

How much rest were they getting? I knew the rapper Sean 'Puffy' Combs had tried to slip us the okie-doke when he said, "sleep is for suckas". On the contrary, I learned that during sleep, the body, repairs, restores, and even the cells regenerate.

How often did they get to see their family and friends?

How often did they get to take a vacation?

How did their body feel, what were they eating, and when?

Did they even like people they worked with or the work?

Then I stopped worrying about *them* and turned the questions inward. I began to ponder whether I could do what I loved and still have enough money to handle my responsibilities, would I still keep the same job? The answer was a solid no. I knew I needed to find a comfortable balance between being and doing.

I pretty much had the doing part 'on lock…' that being part though…yikes! A suggestion to meditate, listen for divine inspiration (gut instinct), take action by putting the foundation and framework into place (the DOING part) and then…gulp…just let it be what it is going to be. I mean, what kind of insanity was this?! This must be a joke. It took a few weeks for me to sit with it but slowly and surely, I began to get it! I mean, it did make a lot of sense. Technically, I was controlling the items that I could control and letting The Creator handle the rest.

Wasn't that what faith was about, after all? The key was not to be tied to any specific outcome, to do as much as I could, then let it go…expecting that the best was yet to come! Therein lay the concept of rest, resting in the knowledge that everything would turn out as it should — the best being bigger, more awesome, more exciting, and more amazing than my original plan. Honestly, I'm still working on it and, depending on the day, am better at one or the other.

The phrase work harder, not smarter, also aligned with this concept. Why work 40+ hours a week when you can get the same outcome and money for less time? Here, I was learning only to take "inspired action," and most times, those "inspired nudges" came when I took the time to pray and meditate. The question became, how much time could I take to rest and get centered if I was out here hustling and grinding with no sleep, in a situation I loathed? The answer is a resounding, none!

Forgiveness

Man, the other dreaded "F-Word!" I knew how hard that one could be. I'd already, slowly, but surely, begun ticking the names of people who I thought had done me dirty off of my forgiveness list – most importantly acknowledging my name at the tippy-top. First, I had to forgive myself for some major missteps - my abortions. I had suppressed the entire experience for more than 20-years, but through my self-discovery work, I realized that trauma still existed deep within my womb. One day, while participating in one of Dr. Vikki's empowerment conference calls, she began sharing how important it was for anyone who'd had an abortion to ask for forgiveness from the spirit of our children and, more importantly, from ourselves. That we'd made those decisions based on the circumstances and support we'd had at the time, it was time to free ourselves from that burden and find ways to honor their spirits. So, I got three stones designating one each for Hunter, Skye, and Bailey and placed them on my ancestral altar. They had already forgiven me and now I just needed to release myself from the mental and emotional bondage. Just like I could with Granddaddy and Grandmommy, I could also ask for guidance from the spirits of my children.

I've never considered such a notion that I could release myself from bondage. My former value system proclaimed that I needed to look

177

to someone else to forgive me. On the issue of abortion and issues related to sexuality and sensuality, they espoused guilt, condemnation, and shame, especially towards women. I immediately liberated myself from this shackle that I'd worn for decades and felt the greatest sense of peace that I'd felt in a long time. I could hardly contain my excitement for this new awareness and wanted to share my journey with everyone I knew.

The Goddess Awakening & Healing Summit

Between 2012 and 2017, I became intrigued by how integrative (aka holistic = mind, body, and spirit) approaches could support the body with its intended design, to more naturally heal on its own. I loved the fact that Functional Medicine sought to find out *why (root cause)* we have an issue versus the traditional *what (diagnosis)* Western Medicine approach that we've all become accustomed to - one-size-fits-all medicine and surgery. I'd sit in my house for hours, mostly studying spirituality-related topics. Then I began attracting a large amount of obscure information regarding the healthcare industry. I was learning about the disparities in health care, specifically in the black community and amongst women in childbirth. I learned about the implicit bias in the health care system and ways to address it through information and advocacy.

I'd been pretty successful at incorporating this new way of operating into my life. I was learning a great deal of new information. With this new learning, I had to deprogram. I had to release myself from decades of clinging to the principles of a value system that I had outgrown. One morning, I was online, viewing a popular health and wellness summit while washing my hair. It was a welcomed distraction because washing and re-twisting locs had become a laborious task. The summit took place over nine days. After the introduction of each speaker, I kept waiting for someone to even remotely look like me. I became so frustrated and questioned why the summit conveners had not found any experts of color to participate? I knew that my family, friends, and colleagues could benefit from this type of information. I also questioned why this life-saving data wasn't more widely available to every human being, regardless of race, class, or *perceived* socioeconomic status. Just then, a voice in my head said… "Well, why don't YOU create it?" I scoffed at the notion at first, I mean really…*how* in the heck was I supposed to create a healing summit? I looked at myself in the mirror, holding a handful of wet locs, *who* was I? I didn't have the platform nor the resources for such a task as this. Just as I was talking myself out of the idea…I remembered that an old colleague once told me that if you don't have a seat at the table, *you* are the meal. Duh!!! Yes, I did have the resources…human resources. I knew some of the wisest and powerful women in the world. They each had a unique perspective as melanated women living in the US. So, just like that, right there in my bathroom mirror, ***The Goddess Awakening & Healing Summit*** was born…in my head anyway!

Once that idea grabbed me, I could not shake it. My fabulous, keep-me-up-at-night idea was both scaring and exciting me. I imagined the infinite possibilities of such an event, and then in typical Wendi-fashion, I made up all of the ways it could not work. Eventually, I shared my idea with my sister-friend, and confidante, Anisha, and not only did she get it, but she was also totally on board to help me bring it to fruition! We immediately started designing our social platforms, collateral, URL, and logo. In less than a week, all five of the speakers, a diverse group of powerful, intentional, and unapologetic, melanated women, who I called "The Dream Team," - said YES to being on the panel!

We intended to have "The Dream Team" share seven days of mind-shifting, information on how women could recognize themselves as *Goddesses, awaken* from the fog and pressures of society and *heal* themselves; which in turn would bring healing to their families for generations to come! I wanted them to experience the transformation that was (is) taking place in my life.

This information was to be shared for one week and include the following topics:

Topic: *"Womb and Sexual Health and Pleasure"* with Thema Azize Serwa, Founder, The Womb Sauna

Topic: *"Healing Past Traumas and Knowing Your Worth"* with Dr. Vikki Johnson, Visionary Soul Wealth

Topic: *"Eating Yourself Sexy"* with Celebrity Chef, Chef Lauren Von Der Pool

Topic: *"Identity Matters"* with Gina Paige, Co-Founder, AfricanAncestry.com

Topic: *"The Importance of Detoxification"* with Dr. Sakiliba Mines, Medical Director, The Institute of Multidimensional Medicine

My vision was huge. I even had my eye on Iyanla Vanzant to offer the keynote. As we know, though, The Creator's timing is divine and, while we had the energy, vision, and excitement, small road-blocks delayed the launch. I loved studying about health and wellness but was still working full time, outside of my passion and still trying to figure out what I wanted to be when I grew up.

Lisa Marie

By December 2016, I was moving for the 10th time since being in the DMV. This time though, I was moving into my own crib and was thrilled about it. Boxes and crap were everywhere, and even though I felt overwhelmed, I couldn't wait for move-in day. It had been a long time coming, and my new condo was the perfect size, price, and in a great, central location. To pass the time while packing, I'd gotten used to listening to esoteric information about health and spirituality via YouTube, mainly searching for information on how to heal fibroids naturally. This particular time, I wasn't actually watching, just listening to video after video to distract me while I was sifting and sorting. When the video I'd been listening to went off, and the next one came on, I instantly became intrigued by this thick, New York accent coming from my computer. Who was this? I thought to myself and went over to my laptop to see a beautiful, chocolate-colored sister sitting on her floor, sharing her thoughts on the energy of fibroids.

Some of the information sounded similar to the things that Thema shared. I soon realized that this video was five or six-years-old. So, I scrolled through and found the most current video that she'd posted only a few hours before. I clicked-through and instantly what she said, drew me in. Before this, she had been called by another name, Nubia I, and had decided that she wanted to go back to using her birth name, Lisa Marie. Being caught off-guard by the fact that people dared to be upset because she wanted to use the name that her mother had given her at birth. She explained that the old name was reflective of a different time in her life and that she felt more like Lisa Maris, as she was growing older. In this video, she was capturing her move from California to North Carolina live on YouTube as she drove. I, too, was in the middle of packing to move, so she became the backdrop of my entire packing experience, getting rid of the old and being open to what awaited me in the new. How synchronistic was that?

She was so insightful, and I spent the next two weeks packing, listening, absorbing, co-signing, and having a-ha moments. I was so grateful to have connected with this Sister…at least via YouTube. I was toggling between her older and current videos, which spanned nine years. I enjoyed learning and watching her be so transparent about the changes that were going on in her life. She seemed determined not to let the opinions of others sway her; which was something that I was releasing myself of too. So, she was modeling what it looked like on the other side of those shackles that I'd wrapped my own ankles and wrists in, both emotionally, spiritually, and energetically.

To my delight, in one of her older videos, she revealed that she too, had done the African Ancestry, DNA test. Her results showed that she descended from the Mafa people living in the Extreme North region of Cameroon - the same ethnic group in which I belonged. I was so excited because I had just returned two months prior from Cameroon and had brought back lots of gifts. So, I immediately mailed her something from our maternal ancestral home. From the very first time I heard her voice and immersed myself in her lessons, I instantly knew that she was from my tribe - literally. This would mark the beginning of the year-long odyssey of personal transformation.

2017: The Year of New Beginnings

My greatest period of transformation came in 2017. Up to that point, I'd read several books, watched numerous lectures, and attended all of the workshops, but now it was time for me to activate. As they say, faith without works is dead. So far, it was the most challenging year of growth I'd ever experienced! Sure enough, as it turned out since 2016 was the year of endings, I went back to the numbers and found that the year 2017 was a journey of change, new beginnings, independence, and becoming my authentic self.

Since the year was **2017**, the calculation was:

$$2 + 0 + 1 + 7 = 10 = 1$$

Here were the main take-aways that spoke to me from Numerologist, Christine DeLorey's article[48] about the year **2017**.

- The One (1) Year is the first year of a brand-new nine-year cycle of your life.

- One is the number of *self*, and I would gain much greater self-awareness, learn about my individuality, and the vital changes that must take place *within me* if I were to attain what I needed.

- The One (1) Year was a time of new interests, experiences, goals, and understandings about my life, where I'd been, my current situation, and where I wanted to go.

- It was urging me to create a more satisfying existence by recognizing the *new* potential that was developing. It was to be a time of change and new beginnings.

- The past was over, and I needed to fully release the feelings and beliefs that anchored me to it.

You didn't have to tell me twice. I was excited and nervous about the possibilities, but fully expected that everything would turn out just as I'd envisioned it would. After a lot of prayer and meditation, I made up my mind to fully embody and harness the energy of the spirit of new beginnings. Most importantly, as the year progressed, I found lots of peace, joy, self-love, healing, and emotional stability.

Pitch the Panties

As the owner of the Black Berry Beauty Academy[49], Lisa Marie used her 20+ years of experience to teach classes sharing her interpretation of Queen Afua's *The Sacred Woman.*[50] I was so excited because I knew that Queen Afua was responsible for helping women to heal, specifically womb-related issues. So, I took my first class with her in the summer of 2017, and my life was changed, yet again. Each night, our class met online while she shared her brand of the information and the modifications she had made over the years that contributed to her healthy state of being.

Our homework was to wear only skirts and dresses the entire summer and to pitch the panties. Y'all heard that right! …She had us out in these streets with no panties on! How hilarious is that? I know, I know…I'm late on this one 'cause I know many of y'all been going pantyless for years. However, as Lisa Marie began to explain the reason behind this specific lesson, the church girl in me both clutched her proverbial pearls *and* took out her notebook to jot down some notes. It turns out this particular exercise became one of the most fun of the entire class.

She explained that we radiate more feminine energy when we wear skirts and dresses and that wearing pants automatically gives us a more masculine posture. As usual, Lisa Marie was spot-on. According to fashion designer Joseph Altuzarra, "The women's pantsuit for a long time was trying to emulate a menswear staple, and it was about hiding our femininity."[51] Remember the boxy "Power Suites" of the '80s and the recent resurgence of women in pantsuits during Hillary Clinton's 2016 presidential run? I was learning that it was beneficial to invoke my feminine energy in certain situations versus always leading from a masculine one.

I admit I wasn't a frequent dress wearer. So, I went on a shopping spree and collected some of the cutest long and short dresses and skirts. I was committed to doing whatever was needed to discover and harness my feminine energy at a new level. Admittedly, the first few days were awkward as I moved about my day clothed with no draws on. I smirked to myself as I paraded, commando down the produce aisle in Target. As the days passed, I began to relax into the exercise and could feel the shift. I already knew that I was cute but feeling cute *and* feeling feminine *and* sensual are two entirely different things. I was shooting for the latter. Realistically, there are one million cute girls in Washington, D.C. alone so, me being cute *and* smart *and* funny with my own business, home, *and* car wasn't anything out of the ordinary; it was par-for-the-course. I had to tighten up energetically.

On one particular balmy, summer night, I headed to a party on the rooftop of The Ivy City Smokehouse, with my sister-friend, Anisha. Wearing a long red skirt, black tank top, fully-adorned with bracelets, and baubles, and such, I ascended to the roof in all of my feminine glory, feeling sensual and confident. Hell, I'd even placed my favorite Egyptian Musk oil on all of my pressure points - behind my ears, knees, and on my wrists for good measure. So, as you can tell, in the spirit of Beyonce, I did not come to play with them h*es. The night couldn't have been more perfect, the DJ was on point, the crowd came to party, and the humidity in the air made my skin look supple and dewy. Before I could fully cross the threshold, someone grabbed my hand to dance. Now, usually, I would have pulled away in protest, especially if I felt any type of aggression; however, I was trying something new. At the end of the day, it was just a damn dance! So, I moved with him to the dance floor with an open heart and mind.

The dance was cool, and before I could make my way to the bar for a drink of water, someone else grabbed my waist. I turned towards him and just went with it. I mean how you not gonna dance to Luther's "Never Too Much?" The vibe was like dancing in Mommy's living room all over again. The DJ was playing the songs we'd all grown up on, and every time the next beat dropped, every person on the dance floor, would put one hand over their heart and the other cupped hand over their mouth and yell..." Ooooooh!" Everyone was singing along like they'd been transported back into their childhood living room, dancing with their family, to the records on the stereo on a Saturday night.

Lisa Marie was on to something because, throughout the night, I could tell the difference. I got lots of compliments, drink and dance offers. A brotha, I'd seen hanging back in the shadows on many occasions, finally asked for and got my phone number. He told me that he'd noticed me over the years but had finally decided to ask for the digits. I was making my way through the crowd to find Anisha when an old friend grabbed my hand and lead me back onto the dance floor...both Jay Z fans, we'd heard that familiar intro to his "U Don't Know."

"Turn my music high, high, high, higher."

"...You don't know what you do..."

"Sure I do...!"

No matter how many times I heard that beat drop, it got me hyped. The words were so apropos for the moment, *"...you don't know what you... sure I do"* ...I smirked to myself, sure I do. I am clear what is going on here. I allowed him to dance a little closer than usual, remembering to go with the flow.

Once I'd finally gotten the chance to come up for air, I began sharing my experiment with Anisha. My old friend came and took my drink order and made his way to the bar. Anisha looked at me and said, "Dang, Sis, you done brought all the boys to the yard tonight!" We both cracked up laughing, but it was true. My energy was electric. It was just another fantastic Lisa Marie lesson that reminded me to shake off the old rigid energy of low self-esteem and to tap into that of the Divine Feminine. The sensual Goddess that   I   was   born   to   be   unapologetically.

The homie came back with the drink. He offered to escort me to my car, located in a dark alley on the other side of the block. I certainly had no business parking over there, so I was grateful for the offer. We caught up on family and life during our walk, and once safely fastened in, I rolled down the window, and he leaned in for a few kisses. Yawn…I knew it was coming. He was so predictable. I also knew I had no interest, having been down that road with him years before. I just enjoyed the smooch with no attachment, merely allowing it to be a reminder that there was something to be said for the feminine allure and that I could choose to harness at any time.

I continued the homework throughout the summer and experienced many revelations. I became more self-aware of the energy that I was putting out. I was intentional about releasing the highest vibration so that I could attract at that same level. I kept questioning why it took me so long to come to this awareness. I chalked it up to the fact that I was in the right place at the right time, and more than that, I was grateful.

Sticky Rice & Tears: A Reflection

The year 2017 was one of the most impactful years of my personal and spiritual growth. I decided that I needed to get away, a change of scenery, the spirit of Wandering Wendi had kicked in strongly, and I was ready to explore.

Below are two excerpts from my blog, FromJerZtoMe.com, I documented my solo trek to Bangkok, Thailand, Bali, Indonesia, Kuala Lumpur, Malaysia, and Beijing, China.[52]

The First Leg

July 12, 2017

"My brain is usually buzzing 100 miles per minute, juggling bits of information, random thoughts, fresh ideas, memories, and such. I knew that I wanted to travel during my summer vacation while Sydni was at Camp Grandma. I had a few ideas but wasn't 100% clear on the final destination.

I knew I needed to quiet my brain, really think about it, listen to my heart and go ahead and pick something already. Part of the lesson on my trip was not to be so rigid, and inflexible; to just go with the flow. So, once I got crystal clear and zeroed in on Thailand, everything began to fall right into place. Seriously, it almost felt too good to be true.

It started a bit rocky with a 2-hour delay from D.C. to Beijing, causing us to miss our connection to Bangkok. So, instead, I chilled and took an amazingly relaxing bubble bath in my beautiful hotel room in China. I kept thinking, wowzers, I am taking an amazingly relaxing bubble bath in this dope ass hotel in China. Get. It. Girl!

Day Four

"I am on day four of being on my solo travel throughout South East Asia. I am excited to be traveling alone, learning about myself, other people, and cultures. This trip was destiny! A few months ago, I just started talking about wanting to visit Thailand. Everything worked out easily, I 'attracted' a cheap flight, a wonderful Airbnb host, and amazing 'strangers' have been coming together to assist me on my 14-day journey.

Notice I used the word 'attracted'. I am a firm believer that we all can co-create our lives and our experiences. I have been putting this into practice for the last few years with much success. I said that I wanted to travel, buy a home, and become an entrepreneur and BOOM! ...I have manifested each one! Obvi, I am still working on ticking a few more items off of my vision board, but you catch my drift.

I visited the temples in downtown yesterday, taking it easy today; I took the train to explore more of Bangkok. It was safe, quick, cheap, clean, and easy to navigate.

My Airbnb host, Anne, is amazing. She was the first one to pop up in the app so, I contacted her, and she quickly responded with all of my options. She has treated me so well. Over the last three meals, we have discussed Thai and Western culture, black skin, and my locs (inevitable), boys (inevitable), politics, and living our passion. Anne is an amazing fashion designer of clothing, swimwear, and interiors and teaches it at the local university. We stayed up late each night, chatting like old friends!

In my attempt to remain present and in the moment, I found myself getting a bit teary-eyed while dining at Eat Thai at the Central Market (...a huge shopping mall here in Bangkok.) I was giving thanks to The Creator for allowing me to manifest such a wonderful trip. I was wondering what Granddaddy, Grandmommy, Auntie, and Uncle George were thinking about me rolling solo. I was thinking about how much fun I was having, solo, eating, and exploring on my own time. It is rare for me not to have something on my schedule. Here, I can wake up when I want, go to sleep when I want, move around when and where I want - whenever I want. Cool huh?

I was giving thanks for the amazing pad thai, mango, and sticky rice that I was enjoying. Never mind that I am gluten sensitive, and I knew my stomach would be on bubble in T-minus 7 seconds. Hell, YOLO (you only live once) so, I crushed it and kept it pushing.

The overall point is that you can create the life you want. Once I became more in-tune with my own heart and desires AND allowed myself the opportunity to dream big dreams; things started to come together. Of course, I've had to let a lot of people and situations go to manifest this, but it has been worth it. I can't wait to see what amazement awaits me on the next stop on the journey #FromJerZtoMe!

This was an amazing trip. I learned how to trust my intuition, intellect, and allow myself to flow at the moment while traipsing solo in Southeast Asia. It was freeing, and I plan on doing it again soon. I also learned that, though I love traveling, I didn't have to trek half-way across the world, solo, to find myself. I am always right here. The work happens in the mirror, and I decided that it was time to stop running and buckle down if I was serious about my awakening and healing. As I encountered one layer, like an onion, new emotions, hurts, and things that needed addressing and healing were emerging. I promised to dig in and flow with it, if not for me, then for the seven generations to come.

The Zen Palace: Manifesting the Vision

During this time, my professional life was causing me so much stress that my doctor put me on medical leave twice in 6 months. I was still purging and preparing myself for my move. Ironically, Lisa Marie was changing yet again, and watching her navigate the process, gave me the courage to become unapologetic about my evolution. I was enjoying her teaching style and the quantum leaps I was making in my life under her guidance and wanted more. I quickly signed up for her next class called Sacred Space, where she taught us how to decorate our homes using an African version of what is popularly known as Feng Shui, incorporating African principles and inspiration. I'd always told myself that I was not creative. Therefore, this was my opportunity to push past that lie and create the Zen-like environment that I wanted to live in.

Lisa Marie helped our class understand the importance of having a positive flow of energy in our homes. She broke down the meaning of the different cardinal (N, S, E, W) directions and how vital plants were in helping to purify the room in addition to providing beauty. She taught that though it was convenient to hire somebody to occasionally clean, it was healing and beneficial for us to clean our own homes so that we were familiar with every nook and cranny of it. She suggested that we throw away broken dishes and kitchen utensils because keeping them energetically implied that we were afraid of lack and that we couldn't attract new usable items by holding on to old broken ones. She also talked about what different colors meant and the placement of the furniture in each room. All around, it was an educational and enlightening experience. I was so grateful that Thema helped me clarify my vision of my living space within myself for The Creator to be clear enough to give me what I asked. I was also grateful for Lisa Marie's guidance on how to enhance the space…I call it The Zen Palace. Every guest who walks in the door remarks about how peaceful and beautiful the space feels – just as I intentionally designed it.

Lisa Marie also talked about the importance of detoxification, which I'd already added to my healing regimen, under the medical guidance of Dr. Mines. Spiritual baths, plenty of sunshine, exercise, rest, and lots of water became my non-negotiables. Occasional fasting was also a key element to health and vitality, because in addition to being a spiritual tool, it also gave the body a chance to rest from the hard work of digestion. I'd begun fasting at the age of 10 as a fundraiser for my church then fasted every Wednesday throughout college as a part of my gospel choir so, I was very familiar with the process. Using these tools, I began to feel more vibrant, my skin glowed, and I was full of energy.

Breaking Old Patterns

As early as the fourth grade, I'd always dreaded turning the clocks back as Daylight Savings Time ended. I loathed being cold and the fact it got dark around four o'clock during the winter months. In 2018, I was excited when Lisa Marie agreed to come on my nationally distributed radio show, *The Sanctuary Radio Show*, to share tools for navigating the change of the seasons, both environmental and personal. Years prior, I had diagnosed myself with a very mild form of Seasonal Affective Disorder,[53] otherwise known as SAD. SAD is a type of depression that comes and goes with the seasons, typically starting in the late fall and early winter and going away during the spring and summer. I felt like a vibrant, energized, butterfly in the spring and summer months. On the other hand, during the winter months, I felt like a weepy, bump-on-a-log, and I just wanted to stay in bed and hibernate like a bear. Lisa Marie gave the listeners and me the tools on how to flow effortlessly with the change of seasons versus being resistant. I soared through fall and winter 2018, like a pro. I used the time to go within. To hibernate as it were, get plenty of rest and be intentional of the financial, emotional, spiritual seeds that I was planting that would blossom during the spring season.

Lisa Marie gave great insight into why it was more beneficial, on many levels, to just go with the flow. Resistance meant that I was opposed to something. I was learning to untie myself from any specific outcome. Now for a control freak like me, that could be difficult. Resistance causes anxiety and stress, which is one of the leading killers of melanated people in the US. According to Dr. Stephen Sinatra of the Heart, MD Institute, "Stress is a measure of your mental and physical resistance to circumstances beyond your control. Stressors are threats, demands, or changes to which you attach special, significant importance, and with which you may struggle or feel uncertainty."

Dr. Sinatra also notes that some of the more common stressors include the following:

- The loss of a vital connection through death or the emotional longing for someone who is unavailable, like a spouse or family member; financial distress (this is also why so many of us stay in jobs we hate),
- Being overworked at work, home or school,
- Caretaking,
- Workplace and personal relationship struggles,
- Divorce; and other fears of loss and inability to meet external demands[54]

Unfortunately, our society and culture have come to normalize so many of those every day stressors, making them a regular part of life. I knew it was crucial to my survival and peace of mind that I made some physical and emotional changes, pronto! First, I had to learn to stop white-knuckling my clipboard…just to do my part and learn to let the chips fall where they may. Secondly, I had to trust that the Universe was working *for* me and *not against* me.

I also learned from Lisa Marie that it was OK to change, even if in mid-stream. I had the right and the privilege to do so sans anyone else's permission. My intuition was to be my primary guidance system, and I could rely on it just like I relied on the GPS in the car. It was safe to follow its direction, especially if I'd meditated and asked my Ancestors to guide me in the right direction. This was new from any other concept taught in my past spiritual system. It was both exciting and scary because I realized that at the end of the day, I was responsible for co-creating my life.

The real question became, what type of energy was I radiating to attract these types of people and experiences into my life? I was drawing these lessons into my life, whether they were negative or positive. I was responsible for all of it – not them over there or even the mythological devil, nope! As I was pointing my one finger at everyone else, the other four fingers were pointing back at me. The upside was that I knew I could always make another choice to do something different. I'm not going to lie; this concept took me a while to grasp and incorporate into my daily existence.

I Like to Move It, Move It

Soon after, I was introduced to belly dancing by a sister named Mayasa Telfair. I'd heard that belly dancing had several health benefits, including stress relief, improved posture, core strength, improved self-confidence, digestive health, and more.[55] Being so hyped, I, along with Chers, went to her class the exact next day. Belly dancing, I would soon learn, was a great way to break up the stagnancy in the womb, which was also another reason that fibroids grow. It was a way to add more sensuality and femininity to the energy I offered. Be clear; this wasn't the traditional belly dancing, you may have seen on TV; Mayasa blended African beats with Caribbean styles including a few old-world moves. I loved it!

Admittedly, the moves did not come naturally, but Mayasa was very patient. There I was, swishing my hips from left to right...then

Mayasa would yell, "Gentle...gentle!" I was trying too hard. Between trying to keep my mid-section, feet, hands, and arms all coordinated with the choreography and breathe, I gave myself a good workout and Mayasa a good laugh! I honestly had no idea how to move like that...even more, in some circles, that style of movement was considered for 'fast women.'

Nevertheless, the way that she taught that class, with so much energy, passion, and amazing music, I was inspired to go weekly. Over a few months, my dance moves got better in addition to the slimming effect it had on my waistline. In her teaching, Mayasa relayed lessons about femininity, energy, and the universal principle of giving and receiving, which eventually translated into the energy I brought out into the real world. I was evolving yet again and gratefully placed these new tools in my energetic tool kit.

Auset Eyowaku

I began wearing my hair natural in 2009 and became a product junkie, scouring YouTube to find information about how to manage my relaxer-free tresses. My hair was naturally soft, curly, dry, and would grow as long as I allowed. I used to joke that my multi-textured hair incorporated my German lineage around the edges and my Cameroonian and Sierra Leonian lineages at the crown. I took the traditional route of braiding my hair to create the popular twist-out and pineapple puffs styles. Once on YouTube, down the rabbit hole, I'd go, searching for any of the natural hair care bloggers with hair similar to mine. I found a beautiful young sister named Taren Guy (Auset Eyowaku). Her 'fro was the most beautiful, fullest, and luxurious 'fro I'd seen since some of the dancers on "Soul Train."

I followed her and a few others for a few years until I got my rhythm and understood how to take care of my hair. So, I lost track of her for a time until she 'randomly' popped up in my YouTube cue. This video caught me off guard because she seemed troubled and not her usual friendly, measured self. It took me a while to go through old videos to catch up. I was able to glean that Auset had recently shifted from life as a natural hair care personality to focus more on spirituality. Sounded familiar...just like Lisa Marie's story of how

193

random-ass YouTube viewers dared to be angry with her, a grown woman for expanding and evolving – in her real life.

Ironically, her most recent video shared information on spirituality, some of the same things I'd been studying, and it seemed like our interests were aligned. We were learning similar material, but Auset was obviously at a much higher level of understanding than me. I watched all of her videos and appreciated her unique way of drilling-down dense and esoteric information in a way that made complete sense, just like a patient teacher. I was one of the early members of her private Facebook group called the Indigo 11 Tribe, where a groundswell of people awakening and hungry for more direction, inspiration, and information gathered. We were at all different levels within the group, but she was accepting and tolerant of everybody.

I also took note of how Auset navigated the uncomfortable space of people trying to test her by saying hateful things in such a public way. On many occasions, I saw people tell her that she was the devil and that she was leading people astray. It was wild to watch, but she too stood firm in her beliefs and didn't change her mind just because somebody thought she should. I excitedly took a few of her classes, where I began to think outside of the box of traditional spiritual teachings. I was grateful that I'd attracted yet another guide who supported me to my next level of awakening and evolution. It was all very empowering, and I felt like, under her tutelage, I learned that the only cost to freedom was ownership, and I'd taken a quantum leap forward of consciousness.

These Sisters all came into my life at different times, during the perfect season and for distinct reasons to support my evolution. The key was that I had to be open to receive this type of information. I'd become so rigid in the past, these lessons at any other time in my life would have fallen on deaf ears, or at the very least, I would have given them a vehement side-eye.

The Butterfly Is I

I'd become engrossed in so many different healing modalities from crystals to moon rituals, to eating a strict diet, to Astrology, to Khemetic Science, to cryptic health-related information, that I became overwhelmed. On some days, I preferred staying holed up in my home, studying my lessons. I was in my head a lot – very ethereal. I realized that I didn't want to tip the scales back into being a sheep, being rigid, conforming to rules, just because someone said it worked for them. I had no true interest in pigeon-holing myself into any one spiritual system; I'd had enough of that. Balance was the key to maintaining a healthy mind, body, and spirit. I preferred to create a hybrid of each of these modalities, just the things that resonated deeply within my spirit. I preferred a more holistic approach to spirituality and in having the power within myself to define what was valuable or not.

Even though sometimes Auset's was speaking above my level of understanding, my favorite part about her teaching style was that she insisted that we go within to examine the information; to ensure that it made sense to us individually. She implored us to get in touch with our own perceptive truth and reality. I refused to be at the allegiance of a specific religious system or person again. **No one was my guru.** I'd attracted great teachers at specific moments in my life for particular circumstances, but I had my own intelligence, guidance system, path, and purpose. The people I attracted into my life, who became my teachers were what I called my, board of directors, simply to guide, support, and offer information for me to consider. Their role was not to force anything on me; what worked for them worked for them, and I was on the path to finding out what worked for me. It was liberating to understand that I had most of the answers within me. For those times I needed more guidance; I could always pray and ask my ancestors, spirits, and guides for more direction.

Right after making that declaration to myself, I went to the park to test the concept that what I spoke into existence would manifest...eventually. I figured I'd start with something easy. So, since I loved butterflies, I set the intention that I would see at least nine butterflies that day. After a couple of hours, I was puzzled because I didn't see a single, solitary one! Actually, over the next week, I only saw ONE. Dang. Butterfly! How in the heck did that happen, I wondered? I had all of these so-called tools and had been deploying them with a high rate of success for other things. How on earth could I not manifest more than one butterfly over a week? That was frustrating, and since I loved looking at them and appreciated their metamorphosis story, I wanted to learn more about the symbolism of the butterfly. So, I took the "Spirit Animal" test by Elena Harris,[56] and what I read was powerful and gave me the chills.

"The butterfly symbolizes personal transformation. When the butterfly comes into your life as spirit guide, you may be going through or expect important changes in your life and internal environment, related to your perspective on a subject, aspects of your personality, or personal habits."

The list below solidified that the butterfly was my spirit animal because, in the last five years, I'd experienced all of the things below:

- Powerful transformation, metamorphosis in my life, and personality,
- Moving through different life cycles,
- Renewal and rebirth,
- Lightness of being, playfulness,
- Elevation from earthly matters, tuning into emotional or spiritual material

Immediately, I realized that once I stopped looking for things outside of myself and realized that **I AM** already beautiful, whole, perfect, and complete, that the butterfly was I! That everything I had been looking for was right there in the mirror. Life changed at that moment. A few weeks after making that butterfly revelation, I went to the park with my sister-friend, Marsha. Would you believe in less than two hours we saw 15 butterflies?! Yep! That's right, and the first one was purple and black, then they started coming like rapid fire. It was almost like a game. I could picture them saying, "Hey, girl, hey, you finally got it!" Just like in *The Wiz* when Glinda, the Good Witch told Dorothy that everything was already within her. It was true, once I realized my self-worth and that everything I needed was within, I could manifest anything I wanted, even 15 butterflies!

I became more confident in my decision-making and clear on what I wanted to manifest next in my life. I knew that I could use my new tools and guidance of others to support me on my journey. However, I was ultimately in charge. I was the co-creator of my life and only needed to use my God-given intelligence, wisdom, instinct, and intellect to take my life to the next level. I decided that I was intent on manifesting more love of self and others!

The Sibs Nation

Amazing how life can change in the blink of an eye! Especially when you are open to the possibilities. I mean, you think life is one way, then BOOM, it changes! That's what happened to me in August of 2017. While driving to work, I did my normal routine of praying and asking The Ancestors to give me yet another amazing day filled with blessings, fun, and abundance. I didn't overthink it. Then just like that, what happened next changed my entire life for the awesome! While perusing Facebook, I found a direct message from a 'stranger' asking me to check my 23andMe.com DNA test account. They claimed that their test results said I was their…dig this…SISTER! Yep, that was my face too. I was sitting at my desk at work and sort'a looked around to see if anyone was looking at me. I'm not sure if I gasped or made any other sound, but I was certainly semi-shocked. To ensure I wasn't bugging or being punked, I immediately called Erinn and ran it by her, just to be sure.

After a bit of sleuthing, we confirmed that indeed, I had been "found" by my new siblings…with an **"s"**! You heard me right! I had not *one* but *two* new siblings – twins, to be exact! How cool was that?! There was no denying because, in addition to the DNA results, they looked a lot like my family members. I called Mommy to tell her the great news! Without skipping a beat, she said, "Well, now there are just more people to love!" That first night, me from the DMV, Erinn from New Jersey and the twins from Texas, talked on Skype until the wee hours of the morning. We gathered in person, for the first time, two months later, and we've been inseparable ever since! I got exactly what I asked for, more people to love! What a blessing!

The Transformation of The Winter Solstice

After such an amazing 2017, I was interested in what else was on the horizon. The year **2018** would be yet another cycle in which I could choose to explore the energy.
Since the year was **2018**, the calculation was:

$$2 + 0 + 1 + 8 = 11 = 11/2$$

The theme was peace, partnerships, and most importantly - LOVE! While reading Felicia Bender's projection[57], I also learned that the number 11 was a Master Number and that while 2018 equals 11 (eleven), it also reflected the energy of the 2 (two).

Other interesting characteristics of the 2018 year were:

- A Master number demands expansion and evolution, yet expansion and evolution most often take place *within*.

- The 11 is a double 1—all about the self, creativity, initiation, independence, innovation, and self-confidence.

- The foundational energy for the 11 is the 2—all about *love*, relating to others, partnership, patience, and being supportive.

- The 11/2 year was all about experiencing intensely challenging circumstances and coming out the other side stronger, more spiritually evolved, and ready to help others.

That sounded like something I could get with. Now, I'm not saying I'd become a pro at understanding Numerology by any stretch of the imagination, but every time I read a forecast, it eventually

198

played out exactly as was predicted. I intended to harness that energy and get everything out of it I could.

I was in New Jersey for the holidays, and the winter solstice[58] was quickly approaching so, I joined a Facebook group called The Feminine Power Movement to honor the occasion. I learned that the word *solstice* comes from Latin *sol* "sun" and *sistere* meaning "to stand still" and it typically occurred around December 21st or 22nd. The winter solstice celebrated the shortest amount of daylight and the longest hours of darkness, in the northern hemisphere, and the rebirth of the sun. In ancient times, solstices were considered important ritualistic days designed to celebrate the changing of the seasons and a new energy [59]. The solstice was symbolic of the birth of the spiritual sun within, *not* the birth of Jesus, who wouldn't be born for centuries to come. Once this religious aspect was introduced, we became conditioned to feel that we were less than divine beings and separate from the creator. The solstice is essentially tied to a personal awakening.

The Feminine Power Movement Facebook group had about 700 participants that night. The instructions were to light a candle, have a journal and a glass of water handy. Throughout the Facebook Live, the moderator would give us prompts, and we would take the time to reflect on them being sure to stay focused on the energy of regeneration, renewal, and self-reflection.

The first prompt was to list the highlights from 2017. In an excerpt from my journal from *December 21, 2017, @ 7:41 PM*, I wrote:

- *I bought a new condo in a new city because I don't cut grass or shovel snow. It is my safe haven. I love each room, nook, and cranny. I'm grateful!*

- *I escaped from Babylon, aka corporate America, to preserve what remained of my fragile emotional and physical health. I am grateful!*

- *I traveled to Jamaica, China, Bali, Malaysia, Costa Rica, and Thailand on my own personal eat, love, pray adventure.*

- *I learned so much about following my intuition. I am grateful!*

- *My biological twin siblings found me on 23andMe.com. I've got more people to love. I am grateful!*

The next prompt was to think deeply about what I wanted for my future. Honestly, at that point, I had no clue. I'd just ended a contract working for an entertainment company, so I was technically unemployed. I had no idea what I wanted to be when I grew up, so I felt a little out of sorts but still hopeful. As the ladies were posting their answers to the questions, I noticed a woman from Maryland who said that she'd just become a Certified Integrative Health Coach. That piqued my interest, so I in-boxed her to learn more. She told me that she'd just graduated from The Institute of Integrative Nutrition (IIN), which was considered the largest nutrition school in the world. I'd never heard of it before, so I jumped on Google immediately. OMG! I could feel my heart racing and my palms starting to sweat. After reading the description, I realized that was exactly what I wanted to do. I'd begun to enjoy health, especially from an integrative (mind, body, and soul) perspective.

I combed through the entire Web site and watched all of the videos. Then I read the curriculum, which aligned with much of the information that I'd already been studying. Even better, there was an informational call in two weeks, and the next class was beginning in three.

Since I was already journaling, I excitedly wrote the following entry:

9:22 PM

I just felt the inspiration to investigate becoming an integrative health coach. I am on their Web site now and plan to join the info call on 1/10. This could/will be an amazing, life-changing experience. I'm super excited and will travel the world with this knowledge, impacting melanated communities to better health.

The last prompt was to list three things to let go of in 2018:

I wrote:
1. *To stop trying to control everything*
2. *To stop playing small and not standing unapologetically in my power*
3. *To stop procrastinating. I'd learned that procrastination was an abundance killer, and I was doing myself a disservice by not getting that in check.*

I could hardly believe it, in less than two hours, I went from no plan to already visualizing myself starting that class and becoming a health coach. Me joining this Feminine Power Movement call was divinely orchestrated and would help me expand my vision for an upcoming Goddess Awakening & Healing Summit! I was eager to learn more about IIN and what the future held for 2018!

In the spirit of not procrastinating, I, called the school ahead of the schedule information session for January. The journal entry is below:

December 28, 2017 @ 6:59 PM

Life just changed! I'm sweating. I'm hyped. I'm excited. Thank you!
I am officially an IIN student. I'm going to be in training for the next year to be an integrative (holistic) health coach. I will support people on their journey to healing. I wondered why I'd been so attracted to the Winter of Wellness, The Truth About Cancer, and other health-related summits.

My goal is to heal myself and others, targeting my beloved melanated community. I want to help them alleviate stress and become their healthiest and best selves. The virtual classes begin on January 16th.

I'm so excited. It's true that when you sit quietly, the next best-inspired step will come. I paid the tuition in full and will get to write it off on my taxes this year! Aye! Aye!

I never thought I'd be an official student again but life has its way…What an amazing gift to bring in the new year!

Old Things Made New

So, in January of 2018, **The Goddess Awakening & Healing Sanctuary, LLC** was *re-born, re-framed,* and *re-envisioned*! I gave myself the gift of studying full time and devoured the information that the year-long certification class provided me. Ironically, most of the professors were experts that I'd already studied under when I was researching on my own. I absorbed the information with ease and passion. It was exactly what I needed at the time and answered so many questions for me. Anisha was so excited to see "our baby" still growing, she passed me the baton to move the vision forward! I wrote the mission statement in my next Lisa Marie class for budding entrepreneurs.

Mission Statement:

As a Certified Integrative Health Coach, I will educate, inspire, and empower melanated women to unapologetically transform into their most authentic and healthy selves by tapping into the Goddess within.

Logo: I was very intentional when I created my logo, incorporating powerful symbology to match my powerful internal revolution.

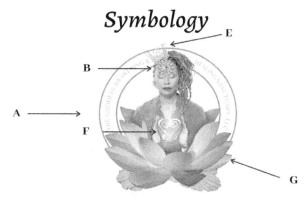

Symbology

A: *Goddess:* The powerful (wo)man we were all born to be but have been socialized and conditioned to have forgotten.

B: *Awakening:* Moving away from the status quo and old ideas, concepts, spiritual systems, relationships, and jobs that don't serve us. Awakening to our passions, destiny, and purpose. Remembering who we are.

C: *Healing:* Breaking free from past traumas, known and unknown, that we have brought on ourselves or that have been passed thru our ancestral line. (i.e., diseases, addictions, generational curses

D: *Sanctuary:* The safe place where I hold space for women to unapologetically cry, laugh, excavate, awaken, attune, align, and activate.

E: *Gold Crown:* A traditional symbolic form of headwear representing power, wisdom, and enlightenment, inspiring knowledge, spirituality, and a deep understanding of the self and the soul.

F: *Sankofa:* A word in the Twi language of Ghana translating to "Go back and get it", associated with the proverb, "It is not too late to go back for that which you have forgotten."

G: *Pink Lotus Flower:* The Lotus closes at night sinking underwater, re-emerging and blooming each morning, symbolizing "rebirth".

I studied the official curriculum and supplemented my studies with more esoteric data related to the health of melanated people, which was my passion. From grappling with my own dis-ease, food allergies, and learning to modify my diet in new ways to benefit my conditions, I began learning more about how food is used as a form of warfare on certain populations worldwide. Food or the lack of it, in certain communities, propelled the incidences of illness and death. I'd had the first-hand experience with having eaten the

Standard American Diet (SAD)[60] that studies confirmed the following:

- If you eat the Standard American Diet,
- Live a sedentary American lifestyle,
- Solely seek medical attention via American Medical Association standards (medicate vs treating root cause),
- Your average life span is *78-years-old.*[61]

This means that mid-life is *39-years-old*, so, since I am way past *39*, I figured, I'd better start enjoying my life NOW!

Though sometimes on information-overload, I was inhaling copious amounts of cryptic information on:

- The Microbiome[62] and how *ALL disease begins in the gut (yep, even cancer, MS, lupus, arthritis, ADHD, Autism, etc.)* and how to potentially *prevent and reverse* it.

- How organic, whole, live food IS the medicine.

- The importance of detoxification of the mind, body, spirit beyond a 5-day, green juice fast. [63]

- The healing properties of essential oils, herbs, and spices.

- Stem cell replacement therapy success stories.[64]

- The dangers of Wi-Fi aka electromagnetic frequency and the toxic environment within our bodies.[65]

I was studying these "lessons" morning, noon, and night, in the shower, in the car, while doing chores. I know, I know…have your eyes glazed over yet?! Though much of this information was cutting-edge technology, physicians were going back to African, Asian, and other ancient methods of healing and commodifying it today. These were the same modalities our great-great-grandmothers used decades and centuries ago that got them slapped with the label of "witch" or a "black magic woman."

Then I read Frederick Douglass' account of *How Slave Owners Used Food as A Weapon of Control* [66] and realized how eerily similar this century-old account was to the state of food consumption in the U.S. in modern times. I was connecting the dots of the concerted effort to keep melanated people "in their place" by using food and religion as two powerful weapons. It was becoming more evident that the traditional Western healthcare industry wasn't about the healing of its citizens. Rather it was more about reaping financial gain from those of us, they considered consumers – those they kept addicted to pharmaceutical drugs. It was both disheartening and despicable at the levels of deception both of these "industries" were employing against us.

The Sanctuary Radio Show

Between studying, being a mom, and trying to carve out some type of social life, 2018 proved to be one of the most fulfilling years up to now. Though I was already hosting small-scale Goddess Gatherings for private clients, schools, and corporations, I still wanted to share this important information on a larger scale. As fate would have it, I was hanging backstage at an event in Washington, D.C. I ran into Maxx Myrick, an award-winning air personality and radio programmer, who was now at D.C.'s Office of Cable Television, Film, Music, and Entertainment serving as the General Manager of DC Radio.gov, 96.3 HD-4. This was the newly-created District of Columbia's first and official government radio station, in partnership with Howard University's WHUR. We were casually talking about the new radio station, and once he confirmed there was no health-related show already in the works. I asked him if I could host one.

Now to be clear, I had no idea what that entailed. I was only asking in jest and didn't think he would say yes. He suggested I submit a proposal. Uh, oh! What had I gotten myself into? Now I had to create a proposal. Gratefully, my network is large and wide, and I asked some of my former interns and students to help me create one.

Within no time, the show ideas were flowing down like a river. By the time I realized it, I'd had five fully-fleshed out show ideas and a yes from my proposed guests. I was enthusiastic and uneasy. I knew I wanted to talk about some pretty unique topics and wasn't sure how they'd be received.

I called it *The Sanctuary Radio Show*, a spin-off of my coaching practice. My vision was to address the well-documented, health and wellness disparities faced by melanated peoples, specifically women. I wanted to share long-lost, indigenous, holistic methods of healing our bodies with a focus on nutrition; while highlighting local change-agents who are contributing to positively impacting the trajectory of the community.

My pitch meeting with Maxx was direct and to the point. He green-lighted my proposal, and I was off to the races. I called on some of the people who had guided me on my evolutionary path. There were so many powerful and wise people to choose from right here in my local area. On July 11, 2018, I taped my first episode of *The Sanctuary Radio Show* in the D.C. studios of The Office of Cable Television, Film, Music, and Entertainment. There was no question that I had to have my mentor and Big Sister, Dr. Vikki Johnson as the inaugural guest. She shared the importance of Soul Wealth, sacred sisterhood, and the transformation that can take place when a woman leads. I also called on all of my favorites, Risikat, Thema, and Lisa Marie, to share their wisdom with the listeners.

The topics were intended to inspire, inform, and educate the listeners and included:

- **Episode 2:** Growing Your Own Food and Using it as Medicine with Dr. Linda Thompson

- **Episode 6:** The Power of the Womb: A Twerk A Day Keeps the Fibroids Away

- **Episode 15:** The Journey to Womanhood: The Importance of Rites of Passage Ceremonies with Marcia Wright, Esq.

- **Episode 20:** Yes, Black Does Crack: The State of Black Women's Health with Dr. Jasmine Abrams

- **Episode 29:** The Energy of Healing with Dr. Nazirahk Amen

- **Episode 35:** The Effects of Perpetual Traumatic Slavery Disorder with Dr. Patricia Newton (PTSD)

I was blessed to have my friends, Kia Bennett, Tamara Wellons, and Elise Perry to agree to let me use their song, "Love You," which was produced by hitmaker, Osunlade, as the show opener. Every time I stepped into the recording studio, I became both anxious and excited yet honored and privileged to be able to share this information. I felt like I was working in my passions and gifts and energetically, standing in the essence of Kora, the Jali, sharing the good news with the people. The response was so positive. I taped 38 episodes in the first season! I remain very proud of the work I produced during that time. Not only did I get to fulfill the vision for my Goddess Awakening and Healing Summit, but this platform also allowed it to evolve and provided the resources to take it to the next level! That was the perfect way to end 2018!

Finally, in January 2019, I officially graduated and became a Certified Integrative Nutrition Health Coach!

Not one to rest on my laurels, with this knowledge, support, and momentum behind me, I was ready to evolve yet again when the opportunity to write a book came my way. Mommy always said that I was a good storyteller and should write a book. I knew that I needed to have a structure in the book-writing process, so I enrolled in a class to keep myself on task. That brings us to this very moment because you are reading my vision manifested.

More Sibs

It turns out, 23andMe.com is the gift that keeps on giving because, again, in January 2019, we "found" two more sisters and even a few cousins! I went from having one sister to having seven! For a total of 10 other siblings! I'd always envied big families, specifically if they all looked alike. So, I could have never imagined in my wildest dream that my desire to have a "rack-of-siblings" would come true, but here we are! Erinn affectionately dubbed us "The Sibs," and now, with our new additions, we've expanded to "The Sibs Nation!" This is still all very new for each of us, and we are creating the blueprint for other families who may have similar situations. It hasn't always been easy, but we are all learning to co-exist and figure out where we fit.

Writing this book was a labor of love. I feel like I birthed another baby. I had to employ the life lessons of going with the flow and trusting the process. I am proud of myself! I know only the best is yet to come on this journey From Jersey to Me!

Sound Scape: "It's My Time" by Kelly Price

Revolucion! Puerto De La Habana, Cuba
Photo: Jacqueline Cofield (August 2016)

My Discoveries & Reflections

The Devil DID NOT Make Me Do It!

What I know for sure is that there is no devil. There is no one to blame things on except for the person in the mirror. Unfortunately, this pertains to things in situations that we know about and that we don't know. It allows tough experiences to happen, which allows us to learn a lesson. Some value systems encourage you to blame everything on the devil instead of standing in your own power. The state you currently find yourself in is due to your actions or inactions. The devil was never holding me back from greater; I was the culprit. Either I didn't love myself enough, or even worse, I didn't feel like I deserved the best of everything.

It's My Time

Together these experiences on my journey From Jersey to Me, have made me the woman I am today. I have come to appreciate the good, bad, and ugly. Though I am still sorting through my fibroid experience, I realize that they persist in encouraging me to dig even deeper, to peer into the mirror more intently to uncover the root and to feel whole and complete in spite of them. The most important part of this is my realization that regardless of what ails me, I am still whole, perfect, and a creation of pure positive energy and love.

Though the work of healing happens in phases, each time you think you've overcome an issue, like an onion, the layers peel back to reveal yet another revelation. The healing work must be done in tandem with the joy and pleasure of living life to the fullest. You absolutely should not get stuck in the healing phase. I have vowed to myself that I will use this last year of my 40's to activate all of my God-given gifts and powers to co-create the life I desire. After all of these lessons, I realize that I am worthy of the best of

EVERYTHING, pleasure, joy, resources, love, fun, pristine health, and much more.

The days of me dimming my shine are over. Like Beyonce reminded me in her song, "Already," from the movie "The Lion King," it's time to shine already! I was the only one holding me back.

"Shine already, it's time already..."

"Shine already, it's time already..."

Don't put all of your trust in the deity, crystal, candle, or guru...you, my dear, are the magic!

It's time to ***AWAKEN, ATTUNE, ALIGN, ACTIVATE, and ALLOW!***

Ase! ...and so it is!

YOUR REFLECTIONS
CHAPTER 8

Are you living your dream?

Yes or no? (circle one)

Do you believe you are doing what The Creator put you on this earth to do?

_____

_____

_____

_____

_____

Have you ever gotten a little tingle in your belly when a great idea *"just popped"* into your head?

Share the details of the vision.

How does it make you feel?

_____

_____

_____

_____

_____

wendicherry.com   @AwakenAndHeal

What steps did you take to make it happen?

If you didn't take any steps, what two steps can you take by month's end to make it happen?

_____
_____
_____
_____
_____

Go back and re-read your vision.
Are you being honest with yourself?
Now go back and expand upon the vision.

_____
_____
_____
_____
_____

Now re-write it BIGGER AND BOLDER!
How does it make you feel?

_____
_____
_____
_____
_____

Like Grandmommy and Auntie used to say, *"If you live and nothing happens,"* you've still got time to get moving to become the best version of you for the new year.

What two steps can you take by month's end to make it happen?

_____
_____
_____
_____
_____
_____
_____
_____
_____
_____

Conclusion

Healing and awakening is both a private and personal revolution, one that shouldn't be televised. In my opinion, as more people take the brave step of attempting to heal and love themselves more deeply, the vibration of love will automatically be infused into the world. Once you begin to heal, you understand just how powerful, brilliant, and worthy you are. With this knowledge, you can break out of the mental, emotional, and spiritual chains that could potentially be holding you back from being your greatest version. I can vouch for that though this work isn't easy; it is required. Like any revolution, there is a lot of pain before the change. Through the work of my one-woman-revolution, I feel more confident, peaceful, loving, light, and connected!

Does that sound like the type of revolution that you'd fight for? In case you didn't remember… you deserve the best of everything!

Scrapbook

**Mommy & Daddy bringing me home from
the adoption agency (October 1970)**

Me, Grandaddy , and Aimee Dawn

Auntie   **Uncle George**

215

Me and Aimee Dawn

Me, Wanda and Aimee Dawn   **Aimee, Aunt Sylvia, Wanda and Me**
                                      dancing in the living room

Auntie, Sydni, and Me on Eastern Shore, Va. (November, 2003)

Me and Erinn (aka Stis), Circa 1991

Sydni & Mommy, Circa 2003

Me, Sydni, and Mommy at Sydni's 13th Rites of Passage ceremony, Red Bank, NJ Photo: Zoe Tsopelas (November 2016)

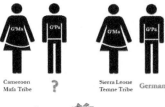

My African Ancestry Family Tree

Naming ceremony at Howard University, June 2015 (Photo: Janaye Ingram)

My Kemetamorphosis standing in the light in the door way of Ramses II in Abu Simbel Temple (Kemet) (July, 2016)

Me in front of my ancestral alter (August, 2018)

Stis, Shawnie P ooh, Me, Shan Shan, Meet
the Sibs DC, (October 7, 2017)

TheSibs Nation, Atlantic City, NJ
(May 18, 2019)

The Mentor's Mentor, Dr. Vikki
Johnson (March, 2019)

List the top 10 things you love and appreciate about yourself.

(*Focus more on who you are as a person versus what you do for a career.)

Example: Great smile, loving, loyal, pretty feet, obnoxious laugh, witty personality

1. _____
2. _____
3. _____
4. _____
5. _____
6. _____
7. _____
8. _____
9. _____
10. _____

wendicherry.com   @AwakenAndHeal

Love Letter to Me

Beloved, Your Name,

You are an awesome wonder, created by God. Everything you have been through up to this point was for your good and not meant to harm you in any way. You may have made some major mistakes on your journey but you did the best you could with the tools you had at the time.

You may have been afraid and acted on pure emotion. It's ok. I forgive you. You didn't lose anything, you merely learned a great lesson. You are pure positive love, powerful beyond measure, and worthy of the best of everything!

I am excited to see where we go next on this journey of evolution and self-discovery.

I love you!

xo,
Your Name

wendicherry.com   @AwakenAndHeal

Daily Journaling

*M*ommy introduced me to journaling in 1978. Occasionally, I review the stories in more than 30 of my journals, to relive the impactful experiences I had on this journey. I fondly remember the victories and use the more painful lessons as a reminder that I am human, I am still learning, and that in the present I can choose to make a more informed choice for my future. Journaling has allowed me to express my deepest thoughts and feelings in a safe and contemplative way.

Use the following prompts as a way to get started. Purchase a journal and commit to at least one entry per day, reviewing them occasionally to identify patterns or blind-spots you may have encountered along the way.

AM: Consider jotting down seven (7) things you love each morning. This allows you to begin the day with a positive vibration and loving energy to carry you throughout your day. After all, the greatest vibration is love!

I always begin my entry with the following:

Thank you: This is my way to thank The Creator for such a wonderful day.

Help Me: I ask for help from my Ancestors, Guides, and Angels to guide me and to keep me and my loved ones protected throughout the day.

Wow: I remember to never take anything for granted and remain in awe at the wonder and beauty of life.

PM: Then seven (7) things you are grateful for each night before bed and anything you just need to get off of your chest.

- This exercise allows you to go to bed with more peace and contentment, which supports our body's natural cycle to restore, regenerate, repair, and renew our cells during sleep.

- Therapy is one of my favorite healing modalities; however if you are currently unable to invest in traditional therapy, write your thoughts onto paper. This exercise allows you to get your emotions *up* and *out* of your body. Bottling up your feelings causes stagnancy and dis-ease within the body. Therefore, the act of writing them onto paper can be very therapeutic.

- In my opinion, the *true* American dream is to sleep peacefully at night!

What are the two action steps you are going to take tomorrow to put your vision into action?

Cheers to the deepest, most restorative, peaceful sleep you've had in years!

About the Author

*W*hen she realized that she was born with all of her Goddess powers already within, Wendi changed her diet, her mindset, her career, and the revolution began.

A Certified Integrative Nutrition Health Coach, producer and host of ***The Sanctuary Radio Show*** on DCRadio.gov, Wendi has been featured nationally and internationally on outlets including ***89.3-WPFW, 93.9-WKYSFM, 96.3-WHUR*** and 104.2-Elle'FM in Cameroon, West Africa and is a contributing writer for the ***AARP Sisters Newsletter***.

When she's not hanging out with her teenage daughter or 'bobbin' her head to some Golden Era hip hop, you can find Wendi enjoying nature. She loves educating, empowering, and inspiring melanated people to unapologetically transform into their most authentic and healthy selves by tapping into the God and Goddess within.

Visit **wendicherry.com** to follow the revolution!

The From Jersey to Me:
The Awakening & Healing of a Goddess Playlist

Click the picture to enjoy the companion Spotify play list
which explores the sound track to Wendi's evolution!

MUSIC IS HEALING

What is on your personal playlist? Write down 5 of your
favorite songs and play them when you need a pick-me-up!

_____

_____

_____

_____

_____

Follow the Revolution

SHARING IS CARING!

Please consider sharing a positive book review on **Amazon** or on **your social media account**. This is a great way for me to build rapport and encourage more readers to consider my work.

#AWAKENANDHEAL

Resource Guide

Queen Afua
Founder
Sacred Women
A pioneer in the green foods movement, Queen Afua is the founder of the Sacred Woman Rites of Passage Program, and the CEO of the Queen Afua Wellness Center.
queenafua.com
@queenafua

Dr. Nazirahk Amen
Naturopathic Doctor, Chinese Medicine Practitioner, Classical Homeopath
The Wisdom Path
Dr. Amen is a naturopathic doctor with 20+ years' experience.
wisdompath.net
@ doctorfarmerbrother

Eurica Huggins-Axom
Co-Founder
African Diaspora Ancestral Commemoration Institute (ADACI)
Helps institutionalize the commemoration of the millions of African ancestors – men, women, and children, who perished during the Middle Passage – the Maafa, and survivors, by creating innovative programs using arts and education as powerful tools for transformation and spiritual development.
adaciancestors.org

Anthony Browder
Founder & Director
IKG Cultural Resources
IKG is an educational organization that is devoted to the re-discovery and application of ancient African history, culture, and wisdom.
ikgculturalresourcecenter.com
@anthonytbrowder

Natalie Cofield
Founder
Walker's Legacy
Walker's Legacy is a global platform for the professional and entrepreneurial multicultural woman that helps women walk into their professional passion and purpose.
walkerslegacy.com
@walkerslegacy

Auset Eyowaku
Certified Reiki Master and Spiritual Guide
The Liberation Code
indigo11group.com
@auset_eyowaku

Lisa Marie Goodson
Founder
The Black Berry Beauty Academy
Offering Ancient African wisdom for the modern sister.
blackberrybeautyacademy.com

Dr. Vikki Johnson
Chaplain, Speaker, Author & Creator
Soul Wealth®
vikkijohnson.com
@allthingsvikki

Dr. Sakiliba Mines
Medical Director
The Institute of Multidimensional Medicine
timmed.com

Dr. Gina Paige
Co-Founder & President
African Ancestry, Inc.
African Ancestry is the world leader in tracing maternal and paternal lineages of African descent, having helped more than 500,000 people re-connect with the roots of their family tree.
africanancestry.com
@africanancestry

Thema Azize Serwa
Founder
The Womb Sauna
thewombsauna.com
@thewombsauna

Ralph Smart
Psychologist. Author. Counselor. Life Coach.
Infinite Waters
A YouTube sensation with 26+ million views, Ralph helps people
become their greatest versions by unlocking their true human potential.
ralphsmart.com
@infinitewaters

Mayasa Telfair
Founder
It's Time for Healing Sanctuary
Experiences include vaginal steaming, massage, vaginal (yoni egg)
weightlifting, womb wellness (reproductive health), full-spectrum doula
services, sensual belly dance, herbalism, essential oils, holistic nutritional
coaching, gun training.
itstimeforhealing.com
@mayasawombtherapist

Erika Totten
Spiritual Life Coach, Pleasure Activist, Facilitator
Unchained Visioning
Erika supports Black, Indigenous, and People of Color in breaking the
mental, emotional, and spiritual chains that hinder us from being exactly
who we're uniquely designed to be.
erikatotten.com
@toliveunchained

Dr. Terry Victor
Holistic, Eco-Friendly, Biological Dentist
thedcdentist.com
@thedcdentist

Movies

KweliTV
kweliTV is an interactive on-demand and live streaming video network offers high-quality documentaries, news programs, original docuseries, educational content and independent films and movies that have been vetted by international film festivals from North America, Europe, Latin America, the Caribbean and Africa. kwelitv.com

A Long and Mighty Walk
Dr. John Henrik Clarke
https://www.youtube.com/watch?v=CZ4jUoHzMP4

Hidden Colors
Tariq Nashim
hiddencolorsfilm.com

Out of Darkness
Amadeuz Christ
Trailer: https://www.youtube.com/watch?v=7odxQ6YqF7o

Citations, Index,
& Resources

1.https://www.ajc.com/news/breaking-atlanta-mayor-announces-new-look-atlanta-child-murders/3LXuKcCzoaIeJkzF0PwBkM/

2. https://www.mayoclinic.org/diseases-conditions/vasovagal-syncope/symptoms-causes/syc-20350527

3. https://psychcentral.com/blog/deconstructing-the-fear-of-rejection-what-are-we-really-afraid-of/

4. https://www.linkedin.com/pulse/i-adopted-my-child-birth-what-do-you-mean-trauma-alex-stavros

5. https://psychcentral.com/blog/emotional-trauma-in-the-womb/

6.https://www.amazon.com/Mother-Daughter-Wisdom-Understanding-Crucial-Daughters/dp/0553380125

7. https://suzanneheyn.com/healing-the-mother-wound/

8. http://www.hyperemesis.org/hyperemesis-gravidarum/

9. https://blog.nativehope.org/how-trauma-gets-passed-down-through-generations

10. https://www.mollylarkin.com/what-is-the-7th-generation-principle-and-why-do-you-need-to-know-about-it-3/

11. https://missingpieces.org/wpcontent/uploads/2017/07/Disenfranchised_Grief_and_Dep ression.pdf

12. https://www.cdc.gov/mmwr/volumes/67/ss/ss6713a1.htm

13. https://www.bundoo.com/articles/what-is-the-milk-let-down-during-breastfeeding/

14. https://www.tamalatravel.com/en/the-history-of-the-kora-instrument/

15. https://www.npr.org/templates/story/story.php?storyId=5614846 [God, the Black Man and the Five Percenters, NPR, August 4, 2006]

16. http://bit.ly/LeavingBlackChurch

17. https://www.timmed.com/

18. http://thewombsauna.com/

19. https://www.zestandharmonycounseling.com/balancing-your-emotions-through-the-passionate-sacral-chakra/

20. https://chopra.com/articles/what-is-ayurveda

21. https://chopra.com/articles/what-is-a-chakra

22. http://www.fibroidrelief.org/uterine-fibroids/what-are-uterine-fibroids/

23. https://youtu.be/v4Hh9c9MubQ [Video: "Super Genes" Deepak Chopra & Rudolph Tanzi, June 1, 2016]

24. http://africanancestry.com/how-it-works/

25. https://www.ebony.com/life/black-travel-cameroon/

26. https://www.africanglobe.net/featured/dr-yosef-ben-jochannan/

27. https://adaciancestors.org

28. https://www.merriam-webster.com/dictionary/diaspora

29. https://cameroontraveler.com/2012/03/16/bimbia-the-historical-nerve-wire-of-cameroon/

30. https://www.crisisgroup.org/africa/central-africa/cameroon/tracks-boko-haram-cameroon

31. http://africanancestry.com/how-it-works/

32. https://www.youtube.com/watch?v=Pw12KGSj53k (Video: Colonialism in 10 Minutes: The Scramble for Africa)

33. https://ikgculturalresourcecenter.com/product-category/books/

34. http://kemetexpert.com/understanding-the-colour-black-in-kemet/

35. https://www.washingtonpost.com/news/the-watch/wp/2016/07/06/alton-sterlings-death-appears-to-be-another-police-shooting-that-was-both-legal-and-preventable/

36. https://www.cnn.com/2017/06/20/us/philando-castile-shooting-dashcam/index.html

37. https://www.theguardian.com/us-news/ng-interactive/2015/jun/01/the-counted-police-killings-us-database#

38. https://dfw.cbslocal.com/2017/07/07/timeline-july-7-dallas-police-ambush/

39. https://www.nytimes.com/2013/07/24/opinion/friedman-egypts-three-revolutions.html?_r=0

40. https://www.merriam-webster.com/dictionary/revolution

41. https://www.theatlantic.com/news/archive/2016/08/colin-kaepernick-protest-nfl/498065/

42. https://www.thedailybeast.com/remembering-civil-rights-heroine-fannie-lou-hamer-im-sick-and-tired-of-being-sick-and-tired

43. https://ikgculturalresourcecenter.com/asa-restoration-project/

44. http://santeriachurch.org/the-orishas/

45. http://numerology.astrologyclub.org/2016-personal-year/

46. http://sacredscribesangelnumbers.blogspot.com/2011/06/angel-number-9.html

47. https://www.merriam-webster.com/dictionary/synchronicity

48. https://www.creativenumerology.com/1-year-cycle/

49. http://www.blackberrybeautyacademy.com/

50. https://queenafua.com/pages/about

51. https://www.hollywoodreporter.com/news/hillary-clintons-dnc-look-return-915505

52. https://fromjerztome.com/post/162866517523/tears-sticky-rice-reflections-i-am-on-day

53. https://www.nimh.nih.gov/health/topics/seasonal-affective-disorder/index.shtml

54. https://heartmdinstitute.com/stress-relief/what-stress-can-do-to-your-body/

55. https://basmati.com/2017/02/22/10-ways-belly-dancing-can-boost-your-health

56. https://www.spiritanimal.info/butterfly-spirit-animal/

57. https://feliciabender.com/2018-a-master-11-2-universal-year-the-overall-theme-is-love/

58. https://www.almanac.com/content/first-day-winter-winter-solstice

59. https://foreverconscious.com/summer-and-winter-solstice-rituals

60. https://draxe.com/health/weight-loss/charts-american-diet/

61. https://www.cdc.gov/nchs/fastats/life-expectancy.htm

62. https://draxe.com/health/gut-health/microbiome/

63. https://detoxdiy.com/benefits-of-detoxing

64. https://www.thehealingmiracle.com/

65. https://theemfguy.com/

66. http://bit.ly/FoodAsWar

From Jersey To Me:

The Awakening & Healing of a Goddess

Wendi Dennine Cherry

Made in the USA
Middletown, DE
03 March 2022

61943141R00146